Python for Google

Master the full range of development features provided by Google App Engine to build and run scalable web applications in Python

Massimiliano Pippi

BIRMINGHAM - MUMBAI

Python for Google App Engine

Copyright © 2015 Packt Publishing

All rights reserved. No part of this book may be reproduced, stored in a retrieval system, or transmitted in any form or by any means, without the prior written permission of the publisher, except in the case of brief quotations embedded in critical articles or reviews.

Every effort has been made in the preparation of this book to ensure the accuracy of the information presented. However, the information contained in this book is sold without warranty, either express or implied. Neither the author nor Packt Publishing, and its dealers and distributors will be held liable for any damages caused or alleged to be caused directly or indirectly by this book.

Packt Publishing has endeavored to provide trademark information about all of the companies and products mentioned in this book by the appropriate use of capitals. However, Packt Publishing cannot guarantee the accuracy of this information.

First published: January 2015

Production reference: 1210115

Published by Packt Publishing Ltd.
Livery Place
35 Livery Street
Birmingham B3 2PB, UK.

ISBN 978-1-78439-819-4

www.packtpub.com

Credits

Author
Massimiliano Pippi

Reviewers
Dom Derrien
Samuel Goebert
Marcos Placona

Commissioning Editor
Taron Pereira

Acquisition Editor
Richard Brookes-Bland

Content Development Editor
Vaibhav Pawar

Technical Editor
Tanmayee Patil

Copy Editors
Deepa Nambiar
Vikrant Phadke
Stuti Srivastava

Project Coordinator
Kranti Berde

Proofreaders
Simran Bhogal
Maria Gould
Ameesha Green
Paul Hindle

Indexer
Priya Sane

Production Coordinator
Nitesh Thakur

Cover Work
Nitesh Thakur

About the Author

Massimiliano Pippi has been a software developer for over 10 years, more than half of which he spent working with scientific visualization and backend software for a private company, using C++ and Qt technologies. He started using Python in 2008 and currently works at Evonove, a small company where he has been leading a number of Python software projects, most of which are based on the Django web framework. He is also an open source advocate and active contributor, documentation fanatic, and speaker at conferences. He writes about Python and other development-related topics at `http://dev.pippi.im`.

About the Reviewers

Dom Derrien is a full-stack web developer who has been defining application environments with a focus on high availability and scalability. He's been in the development field for more than 15 years and has worked for big and small companies and also as an entrepreneur.

He's currently working for the game company Ubisoft Inc., where he defines the next generation services platform for its successful AAA games. To extend the gamer experience on the Web and on mobiles, he provides technical means that are transparent, efficient, and highly flexible.

On receiving the invitation to review this book, after a comparable work for the books *Google App Engine Java and GWT Application Development, Packt Publishing*, he was pleased to share his knowledge about Google App Engine again.

> I want to thank my wife, Sophie, and our sons, Erwan and Goulven, with whom I enjoy a peaceful life in Montréal, Québec, Canada.

Samuel Goebert is a computer science PhD student at Plymouth University, UK. Samuel has over 12 years of experience in software development and associated technologies. For further details about him, check out his LinkedIn profile at www.linkedin.com/in/samuelgoebert.

Marcos Placona grew up in Sao Paulo, Brazil, and started tinkering with web development when 14.400 kbs modems were the coolest thing.

He then eagerly pursued a computer science degree and soon after an opportunity arose on the other side of the Atlantic. In his 20s, he decided to move to England where he worked as a software engineer at a software house. He also started blogging on `www.placona.co.uk`.

Marcos has published and printed articles in several web portals, magazines, and books.

He is currently working as a developer evangelist at Twilio; he actively works with developers and communities to equip and inspire them while making their applications better.

www.PacktPub.com

Support files, eBooks, discount offers, and more

For support files and downloads related to your book, please visit www.PacktPub.com.

Did you know that Packt offers eBook versions of every book published, with PDF and ePub files available? You can upgrade to the eBook version at www.PacktPub.com and as a print book customer, you are entitled to a discount on the eBook copy. Get in touch with us at service@packtpub.com for more details.

At www.PacktPub.com, you can also read a collection of free technical articles, sign up for a range of free newsletters and receive exclusive discounts and offers on Packt books and eBooks.

https://www2.packtpub.com/books/subscription/packtlib

Do you need instant solutions to your IT questions? PacktLib is Packt's online digital book library. Here, you can search, access, and read Packt's entire library of books.

Why subscribe?

- Fully searchable across every book published by Packt
- Copy and paste, print, and bookmark content
- On demand and accessible via a web browser

Free access for Packt account holders

If you have an account with Packt at www.PacktPub.com, you can use this to access PacktLib today and view 9 entirely free books. Simply use your login credentials for immediate access.

To Azzurra and Valerio, thanks for being patient with me. But I also have been patient with you, so I think we're even.

Table of Contents

Preface	**1**
Chapter 1: Getting Started	**7**
The cloud computing stack – SaaS, PaaS, and IaaS	8
Google Cloud Platform	**9**
Hosting + Compute	9
Storage	9
BigQuery	10
Services	10
What Google App Engine does	**11**
The runtime environment	11
The services	12
Making our first Python application	**14**
Download and installation	15
Installing on Windows	15
Installing on Mac OS X	16
Installing on Linux	16
App Engine Launcher	16
Creating the application	19
The app.yaml configuration file	19
The main.py application script	21
Running the development server	22
Uploading the application to App Engine	24
Google Developer Console	**26**
Development Console	27
Summary	**27**

Table of Contents

Chapter 2: A More Complex Application — 29
Experimenting on the Notes application — 29
Authenticating users — 30
HTML templates with Jinja2 — 31
Handling forms — 34
Persisting data in Datastore — 36
- Defining the models — 36
- Basic querying — 38
- Transactions — 40
Using static files — 43
Summary — 48

Chapter 3: Storing and Processing Users' Data — 49
Uploading files to Google Cloud Storage — 50
- Installing Cloud Storage Client Library — 50
- Adding a form to upload images — 51
- Serving files from Cloud Storage — 54
- Serving files through Google's Content Delivery Network — 56
  - Serving images — 56
  - Serving other types of files — 59
Transforming images with the Images service — 60
Processing long jobs with the task queue — 63
Scheduling tasks with Cron — 65
Sending notification e-mails — 66
Receiving users' data as e-mail messages — 67
Summary — 71

Chapter 4: Improving Application Performance — 73
Advanced use of Datastore — 73
- More on properties – arrange composite data with StructuredProperty — 74
- More on queries – save space with projections and optimize iterations with mapping — 77
  - Projection queries — 77
  - Mapping — 78
- NDB asynchronous operations — 79
- Caching — 81
- Backup and restore functionalities — 82
- Indexing — 83
Using Memcache — 85
Breaking our application into modules — 87
Summary — 91

[ii]

Chapter 5: Storing Data in Google Cloud SQL — 93
Creating a Cloud SQL instance — 93
Configuring access — 95
Setting the root password — 97
Connecting to the instance with the MySQL console — 97
Creating the notes database — 97
Creating a dedicated user — 98
Creating tables — 99
Connecting to the instance from our application — 100
Loading and saving data — 104
Using the local MySQL installation for development — 107
Summary — 108

Chapter 6: Using Channels to Implement a Real-time Application — 109
Understanding how the Channel API works — 110
Making our application real time — 112
Implementing the server — 112
The JavaScript code for clients — 115
Tracking connections and disconnections — 124
Summary — 125

Chapter 7: Building an Application with Django — 127
Setting up the local environment — 128
Configuring a virtual environment — 128
Installing dependencies — 130
Rewriting our application using Django 1.7 — 130
Using Google Cloud SQL as a database backend — 132
Creating a reusable application in Django — 135
Views and templates — 136
Authenticating users with Django — 140
Using the ORM and migrations system — 143
Processing forms with the Forms API — 146
Uploading files to Google Cloud Storage — 150
Summary — 154

Chapter 8: Exposing a REST API with Google Cloud Endpoints — 155
- **Reasons to use a REST API** — 156
- **Designing and building the API** — 156
  - Resources, URLs, HTTP verbs, and response code — 156
  - Defining resource representations — 158
- **Implementing API endpoints** — 161
- **Testing the API with API Explorer** — 168
- **Protecting an endpoint with OAuth2** — 170
- **Summary** — 173

Index — 175

Preface

In April 2008, 10,000 developers from all around the world were lucky enough to get an account to access the preview release of Google App Engine, which is a tool designed to let users run their web applications on the same infrastructure Google uses for its own services. Announced during Google's Campfire One event, App Engine was described as something easy to use, easy to scale and free to get started; three design goals that perfectly matched the requirements of a typical tech start-up trying to reduce the time to market.

While other big companies at that time were already offering to lease part of their own infrastructure, selling reliability and scalability in an affordable, pay-per-use fashion, Google set App Engine one step ahead by providing developers with application-building blocks instead of simple access to hardware; it is a hosting model followed by many others later on. The goal of this model is to let developers focus on the code and forget about failing machines, network issues, scalability problems, and performance tuning; the choice of Python as the first programming language supported by App Engine was a natural choice for a tool whose aim is to make writing and running web applications easier.

During the Google I/O event in 2012, Google announced that several other building blocks from its own infrastructure would be made available under the name of Google Cloud Platform, first as a partner program and then as a general availability product. Currently, App Engine is not only a notable member of the Cloud Platform family but also a mature and well-maintained platform, widely adopted and with a huge list of customers' success stories.

This book will teach you how to write and run web applications in Python with App Engine, getting the most out of Google Cloud Platform. Starting with a simple application, you will add more and more features to it, each time with the help of the components and services provided by Google's infrastructure.

What this book covers

Chapter 1, Getting Started, will help you get your hands dirty with a very simple functional Python application running on a production server. The chapter begins with making a survey of Google's cloud infrastructure, showing where App Engine is placed and how it compares to other well-known cloud services. It then walks readers through downloading and installing the runtime for Linux, Windows, and OS X, coding a `Hello, World!` application and deploying it on App Engine. The last part introduces administration consoles both for the development and production servers.

Chapter 2, A More Complex Application, teaches you how to implement a complex web application running on App Engine. It begins with an introduction to the bundled webapp2 framework and possible alternatives; then, you will get in touch with user authentication and form handling and then an introduction to Google's Datastore nonrelational database. The last part shows you how to make HTML pages through templates rendering and how to serve all the static files needed to style the page.

Chapter 3, Storing and Processing Users' Data, will show you how to add more functionalities to the app from the previous chapter. The chapter begins by showing you how to let users upload files using Google Cloud Storage and how to manipulate such files when they contain image data with the Image API. It then introduces you to the task queues used to execute long jobs (such as image manipulation) outside the request process and how to schedule batches of such jobs. The last part shows you how to send and receive e-mails through the Mail API.

Chapter 4, Improving Application Performance, begins by showing how to improve application performance using advanced features of Datastore. It then shows you how to use the cache provided by App Engine and how to break the application into smaller services using Modules.

Chapter 5, Storing Data in Google Cloud SQL, is dedicated to the Google Cloud SQL service. It shows you how to create and manage a database instance and how to connect and perform queries. It then demonstrates how an App Engine application can save and retrieve data and how to use a local MySQL installation during development.

Chapter 6, Using Channels to Implement a Real-time Application, shows you how to make our application real time, in other words, how to update what clients see without reloading the page in the browser. The first part shows how the Channel API works, what happens when a client connects, and what roundtrip of a message is from the server to the client. Then, it shows you how to add a real-time feature to our application from previous chapters.

Chapter 7, Building an Application with Django, teaches you how to build an App Engine application using the Django web framework instead of webapp2. The first part shows you how to configure the local environment for development, and then the application from previous chapters is rewritten using some of the features provided by Django. The last part shows you how to deploy the application on a production server.

Chapter 8, Exposing a REST API with Google Cloud Endpoints, shows you how to rewrite part of our application to expose data through a REST API. The first part explores all the operations needed to set up and configure a project and how to implement a couple of endpoints for our API. The last part shows explores how to add OAuth protection to the API endpoints.

What you need for this book

In order to run the code demonstrated in this book, you need a Python interpreter for version 2.7.x and the App Engine Python SDK as described in the *Download and installation* section from *Chapter 1, Getting Started*.

Additionally, to access the example application once it runs on App Engine, you need a recent version of a web browser such as Google Chrome, Mozilla Firefox, Apple Safari, or Microsoft Internet Explorer.

Who this book is for

If you are a Python programmer who wants to apply your skills to write web applications using Google App Engine and Google Cloud Platform tools and services, this is the book for you. Solid Python programming knowledge is required as well as a basic understanding of the anatomy of a web application. Prior knowledge of Google App Engine is not assumed, nor is any experience with a similar tool required.

By reading this book, you will become familiar with the functionalities provided by Google Cloud Platform with particular reference to Google App Engine, Google Cloud Storage, Google Cloud SQL, and Google Cloud Endpoints at the latest versions available at the time of writing this book.

Conventions

In this book, you will find a number of styles of text that distinguish between different kinds of information. Here are some examples of these styles, and an explanation of their meaning.

Preface

Code words in text are shown as follows: "If a user is already logged in, the `get_current_user()` method returns a `User` object, otherwise it returns `None` parameter".

A block of code is set as follows:

```
import webapp2

class HomePage(webapp2.RequestHandler):
    def get(self):
        self.response.headers['Content-Type'] = 'text/plain'
        self.response.out.write('Hello, World!')

app = webapp2.WSGIApplication([('/', HomePage)], debug=True)
```

New terms and **important words** are shown in bold. Words that you see on the screen, in menus or dialog boxes for example, appear in the text like this: "To create a new application, click the **Create an Application** button."

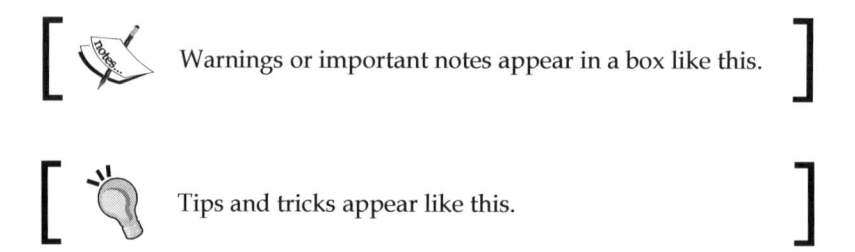

> Warnings or important notes appear in a box like this.

> Tips and tricks appear like this.

Reader feedback

Feedback from our readers is always welcome. Let us know what you think about this book—what you liked or may have disliked. Reader feedback is important for us to develop titles that you really get the most out of. To send us general feedback, simply send an e-mail to `feedback@packtpub.com`, and mention the book title via the subject of your message. If there is a topic that you have expertise in and you are interested in either writing or contributing to a book, see our author guide on `www.packtpub.com/authors`.

Customer support

Now that you are the proud owner of a Packt book, we have a number of things to help you to get the most from your purchase.

Downloading the example code

You can download the example code files for all Packt books you have purchased from your account at http://www.packtpub.com. If you purchased this book elsewhere, you can visit http://www.packtpub.com/support and register to have the files e-mailed directly to you.

Downloading the color images of this book

We also provide you with a PDF file that has color images of the screenshots/diagrams used in this book. The color images will help you better understand the changes in the output. You can download this file from: https://www.packtpub.com/sites/default/files/downloads/B03710_8194OS_Graphics.pdf

Errata

Although we have taken every care to ensure the accuracy of our content, mistakes do happen. If you find a mistake in one of our books—maybe a mistake in the text or the code—we would be grateful if you would report this to us. By doing so, you can save other readers from frustration and help us improve subsequent versions of this book. If you find any errata, please report them by visiting http://www.packtpub.com/submit-errata, selecting your book, clicking on the **Errata Submission Form** link, and entering the details of your errata. Once your errata are verified, your submission will be accepted and the errata will be uploaded on our website, or added to any list of existing errata, under the Errata section of that title.

To view the previously submitted errata, go to https://www.packtpub.com/books/content/support and enter the name of the book in the search field. The required information will appear under the **Errata** section.

Piracy

Piracy of copyright material on the Internet is an ongoing problem across all media. At Packt, we take the protection of our copyright and licenses very seriously. If you come across any illegal copies of our works, in any form, on the Internet, please provide us with the location address or website name immediately so that we can pursue a remedy. Please contact us at copyright@packtpub.com with a link to the suspected pirated material. We appreciate your help in protecting our authors, and our ability to bring you valuable content.

Questions

You can contact us at questions@packtpub.com if you are having a problem with any aspect of the book, and we will do our best to address it.

1
Getting Started

Any software available over the Internet, usually accessed with a web browser, can be addressed as a web application. Social networks, e-commerce sites, e-mail clients, online games are just a few examples of a trend known as web 2.0, which was started in the late 1990s and emerged in the past few years. Today, if we want to provide a service for multiple clients and multiple users, we will likely end in with writing a web application.

Web applications come with an endless list of benefits from a developer's point of view but there is one major drawback to face every time we want to make our software available to other users: we need a remote server connected to the Internet to host the application. This server must be constantly available and respond to clients in a reasonable amount of time, irrespective of the number of clients, or the application won't be usable.

A noteworthy solution to the hosting problem is cloud computing, which is a rather generic term that usually refers to the opportunity to run applications and services on someone else's infrastructure at a reasonable cost and in a way that is simple and quick for the needed resources to be provisioned and released.

In this first chapter we will define in detail the term cloud computing and then introduce the model provided by Google, focusing on the elements that are important to us, as developers, and use them to run our first application using the Google Cloud Platform and Google App Engine.

In this chapter we will cover the following topics:

- A detailed introduction to Google Cloud Platform and Google App Engine
- Setting up an App Engine code environment
- Writing a simple application
- Loading and running the application on a remote server
- Using the administration console

The cloud computing stack – SaaS, PaaS, and IaaS

We can choose to outsource our applications and the hardware they run on, still being responsible for the whole software stack, including the operating system; or, we can simply use existing applications available from another vendor.

We can represent cloud computing as a stack of three different categories: **Software as a Service (SaaS)**, **Platform as a Service (PaaS)**, and **Infrastructure as a Service (IaaS)** as follows:

In the first case, the cloud computing model is defined as IaaS and we basically outsource hardware and every inherent service such as power supply, cooling, networking, and storage systems. We decide how to allocate resources, how many web applications, or database servers we need, whether or not we need to use a load balancer, how to manage backups and so on; the installation, monitoring, and maintenance are under our responsibilities. A notable example of IaaS services are EC2 from Amazon and Rackspace Cloud Hosting.

In the second case, the cloud computing model is defined as SaaS and is the opposite of IaaS since we simply use a turnkey software provided by a third-party vendor, who has no technical knowledge of the infrastructure it runs on; the vendor is responsible for the reliability and security of the product. Notable examples of SaaS are Gmail from Google and Salesforce.

Between IaaS and SaaS we find the PaaS model, which seems to be the most interesting solution from a developer's point of view. A PaaS system provides a platform with which we can build and run our application without worrying about the underlying levels, both hardware and software.

Google Cloud Platform

Google Cloud Platform is designed to offer developers tools and services needed to build and run web applications on Google's reliable and highly scalable infrastructure. The platform consists of several cloud computing products that can be composed and used according to our needs, so it's important to know what these building blocks can do for us, as developers, and how they do so.

As we can learn from the main documentation page at https://cloud.google.com, Google classifies Google Cloud Platform's components into four groups: Hosting + Compute, Storage, Big Data, and services.

Hosting + Compute

There are two options if we want to host an application on Google Cloud Platform:

- **Google App Engine**: This is Google's PaaS and it will be covered in detail later in this chapter.
- **Google Compute Engine**: This is Google's IaaS and lets users run virtual machines on Google's infrastructure with a variety of hardware and software configurations.

Storage

Google Cloud Platform provides several options to store and access users' data:

Google Cloud Storage: This is a highly available and scalable file storage service with versioning and caching. We will learn how to use Cloud Storage in *Chapter 3, Storing and Processing User's Data*.

Google Cloud SQL: This is a fully managed MySQL relational database; replication, security and availability are Google's responsibilities. *Chapter 5, Storing Data in Google Cloud SQL*, is entirely dedicated to this service.

Google Cloud Datastore: This is a managed schemaless database that stores nonrelational data objects called entities; it scales automatically, supports transactions, and can be queried with SQL-like syntax. We will start using it in *Chapter 2, A More Complex Application*, and learn how to get the most out of it in *Chapter 4, Improving Application Performance*.

Getting Started

BigQuery

BigQuery is a tool provided by Google Cloud Platform that allows to perform queries using an SQL-like syntax against a huge amount of data in a matter of seconds. Before it can be analyzed, data must be streamed into BigQuery through its API or uploaded to Google Cloud Storage.

Services

Instead of writing code from scratch, we can easily add functionalities to our applications using some of Google's services through APIs that are very well integrated within Google Cloud Platform:

- **The Translate API**: This can translate text between dozens of languages programmatically, from within our applications.

- **The Prediction API**: This predicts future trends using Google's machine learning algorithms and can be used from within our applications or through a **Representational State Transfer** (**REST**) API. REST is a stateless architecture style that describes how a system can communicate with another through a network; we will delve into more details on REST in *Chapter 8, Exposing a REST API with Google Cloud Endpoints*.

- **Google Cloud Endpoints**: Using this tool, it's easy to create applications that expose REST services, providing also **Denial-of-Service** (**DoS**) protection and **OAuth2** authentication. We will learn how to use them in *Chapter 8, Exposing a REST API with Google Cloud Endpoints*.

- **Google Cloud DNS**: This is global **Domain Name System** (**DNS**) service that runs on Google's infrastructure and provides high volume serving that is programmable from within our applications.

- **Google Cloud Pub/Sub**: This is middleware that provides many-to-many, asynchronous messaging between services that either run on Google Cloud Platform or externally.

All the tools and services provided by Google Cloud Platform are billed with a pay-per-use model so that applications can scale up or down as needed and we only pay for resources we actually use. A handy calculator is provided to have a precise idea of the costs depending on the services and resources we think we will need. Google Cloud Platform offers a certain amount of resources we can use without paying anything; usually, these free quotas are well suited to host web applications with low traffic at no cost.

Chapter 1

What Google App Engine does

As mentioned earlier, App Engine is a PaaS, which means that we have the benefits of SaaS products but with an augmented flexibility as we have complete control over the code. We also have the benefits of an IaaS solution but without the hassle of maintaining and configuring the software environment needed to run applications on a raw hardware system.

Developers are the favored users of a PaaS product such as App Engine because the platform helps them in two ways: it provides an easy way to deploy, scale, tune, and monitor web applications without the need for a system administrator and it offers a set of tools and services that speed up the software development process. Let's explore these two aspects in detail.

The runtime environment

App Engine runs on computing units that are completely managed called instances. We can (and should) ignore which operating system is running on an instance because we interact solely with the runtime environment, which is an abstraction of the operating system that provides resource allocation, computation management, request handling, scaling, and load balancing.

> Developers can choose among four different programming languages to write applications on App Engine: Python, Java, Hypertext Preprocessor (PHP), and Go but we will focus on the Python environment.

Every time a client contacts an application that runs on App Engine, a component of the runtime environment called scheduler selects an instance that can provide a fast response, initializes it with application data if needed, and executes the application with a Python interpreter in a safe, sandboxed environment. The application receives the HTTP request, performs its work, and sends an HTTP response back to the environment. Communication between the runtime environment and the application is performed using the **Web Server Gateway Interface** (**WSGI**) protocol; this means that developers can use any WSGI-compatible web framework in their application.

> WSGI is a specification that describes how a web server communicates with web applications written in Python. It was originally described in PEP-0333 and later updated in PEP-3333, mainly to improve usability under the Python 3.0 release.

The runtime environment is sandboxed to improve security and provide isolation between applications running on the same instance. The interpreter can execute any Python code, import other modules, and access the standard library, provided that it doesn't violate sandbox restrictions. In particular, the interpreter will raise an exception whenever it tries to write to the filesystem, perform network connections, or import extension modules written in the C language. Another isolation mechanism we must be aware of that is provided by sandboxing, prevents an application from overusing an instance by raising an exception whenever the entire request/response cycle lasts more than 60 seconds.

Thanks to sandboxing, the runtime can decide at any given time whether to run an application on one instance or many instances, with requests being spread across all of them depending on the traffic. This capability, together with load balancing and scheduler settings is what makes App Engine really scalable.

Users can easily tune an application's performance by increasing its responsiveness or optimizing costs with a simple and interactive administrative console. We can specify instance performance in terms of memory and CPU limits, the number of idle instances always ready to satisfy a request, and the number of instances dynamically started when the traffic increases. We can also specify the maximum amount of time in milliseconds we tolerate for a pending request and let App Engine adjust the settings automatically.

The services

At first sight, restrictions imposed by the runtime environment might seem too restrictive. In the end, how can developers make something useful without being able to write data on disk, receive incoming network connections, fetch resources from external web applications, or start utility services such as a cache? This is why App Engine provides a set of higher-level APIs/services that can be used by developers to store and cache data or communicate over the Internet.

Some of these services are provided by the Google Cloud Platform as standalone products and are smoothly integrated into App Engine, while some others are only available from within the runtime environment.

The list of available services changes quite often as Google releases new APIs and tools; the following is a subset of tools we will use later in the book in addition to the Datastore, Google Cloud Endpoints, Google Cloud SQL, and Google Cloud Storage services we introduced earlier:

- **Channel**: This API allows applications to create persistent connections with the clients and push data through such connections in real time instead of using polling strategies. Clients must use some JavaScript code to interact with the server. We will learn how to use Channels in *Chapter 6, Using Channels to Implement a Real-time Application*.

- **Datastore backup/restore**: At any given time, it's possible to perform a backup of the entities contained in the Datastore or restore them from a previous backup; management operations are very easy as they can be performed interactively from the administrative console. We will see backup and restore procedures in detail in *Chapter 4, Improving Application Performance*.

- **Images**: This API lets developers access and manipulate image data provided by the application or loaded from Google Cloud Storage. We can get information about the format, size, and colors and perform operations such as resizing, rotating, and cropping and we can convert images between different formats and apply some basic filters provided by the API. We will use some of the features provided by the Images API in *Chapter 3, Storing and Processing Users' Data*.

- **Mail**: This service allows applications to send e-mails on behalf of the administrators or users who are logged in with a Google Account and to receive e-mail messages sent to certain addresses and routed to the application. We will use both these features provided by the service in *Chapter 3, Storing and Processing Users' Data*.

- **Memcache**: This is a general-purpose, distributed memory caching system that can be used to dramatically improve application performance, serving frequently accessed data way faster than accessing a database or an API. We will see how to use Memcache in *Chapter 4, Improving Application Performance*.

- **Modules**: These are used to split applications into logical components that can communicate and share their state with each other. They can be extremely useful as each of them can have different versions and performance and scaling settings, which provide developers with a great level of flexibility when tuning an application. We will see how to use Modules in *Chapter 4, Improving Application Performance*.

- **Scheduled tasks**: This is how App Engine implements the cron jobs. Developers can schedule a job to be executed at a defined date or at regular intervals. Schedules are defined in an English-like format: for example, `every Friday 20:00` is a valid schedule we can use to send weekly reports to our users. We will see how to use scheduled tasks in *Chapter 3, Storing and Processing Users' Data*.

- **Task Queue**: As mentioned earlier, the entire request/response cycle of an application running on App Engine must last at most 60 seconds, making it impossible to perform long operations. This is why the Task Queue API exists--it can perform work outside the user request so that long operations can be executed later in background with 10 minutes to finish. We will see how to use a task queue in *Chapter 3, Storing and Processing Users' Data*.

- **URL Fetch**: As we already know, the runtime environment prevents our application from performing any kind of network connection but accessing external resources through HTTP requests is a common requirement for a web application. This limitation can be overcome using the URL Fetch API to issue HTTP or HTTPS requests and retrieve a response in a scalable and efficient manner.

- **Users**: We can authenticate users within our applications using Google Accounts, accounts in a Google Apps domain, or through OpenID identifiers. Using the Users API our application can determine whether a user is logged in and redirect them to the login page or access their e-mail otherwise. Using this API, developers can delegate to Google or to the OpenID provider the responsibility of creating accounts and verifying the user's data.

For more information on the tools and services provided by Google that we can use from within the App Engine environment, refer to `https://developers.google.com/appengine/features/`.

Making our first Python application

We have now have an idea of the features Google Cloud Platform can provide us with and we are ready to put App Engine in action, but before we can start writing some code, we need to set up our workstation.

Download and installation

To get started, we need to install the Google App Engine SDK for Python for the platform of our choice. The SDK contains all the libraries needed to develop an application and a set of tools to run and test the application in the local environment and deploy it in the production servers. On some platforms, administrative tasks can be performed through a GUI, the Google App Engine Launcher, on other platforms we can use a comprehensive set of command line tools. We will see Google App Engine Launcher in detail later in this chapter.

Before installing the SDK, we have to check whether a working installation of Python 2.7 (version 2.7.8 is the latest at the time of writing this book) is available on our system; we need this specific version of Python because, with 2.5 deprecated now, it is the only version supported by the App Engine platform. If we are using Linux or Mac OS X, we can check the Python version from the terminal that issues the command (notice the capital letter V):

```
python -V
```

The output should look like this:

```
Python 2.7.8
```

If we are on Windows, we can just ensure the right version of Python is listed in the **Programs** section within the **Control Panel**.

The official App Engine download page contains links for all the available SDKs. The following link points directly to the Python version: `https://developers.google.com/appengine/downloads#Google_App_Engine_SDK_for_Python`.

We have to choose the right package for our platform, download the installer, and proceed with the installation.

Installing on Windows

To install the SDK on Windows we have to download the `.msi` file from the App Engine download page, double-click it to launch the installation wizard, and follow the instructions on the screen. Once the install is complete, a shortcut to Google App Engine Launcher will be placed on the desktop as well as an item within the **Start** menu. The Windows version of the SDK does not provide any command-line tool, so we will always use Launcher to manage our applications.

Installing on Mac OS X

To install the SDK on Mac OS X, we have to download the `.dmg` file from the App Engine download page, double-click it to open the disk image, and drag the App Engine icon into the `Applications` folder. It is convenient to keep a shortcut to Launcher in our Dock; to do so, we just have to just drag the App Engine icon again from the `Applications` folder to the dock. The command-line tools will also be installed and during the first execution of Launcher, a pop-up dialog will prompt us as to whether we want to create the symlinks needed to make the tools available system-wide, so they can be executed from any terminal window without further configuration.

Installing on Linux

To install the SDK on Linux and more generally on POSIX-compliant systems, we have to download the `.zip` file from the App Engine download page and extract its contents in a directory of our choice. The archive contains a folder named `google_appengine` that contains the runtime and the command-line tools, and we have to add it to our shell's `PATH` environment variable to make the tools available from within any terminal. The Linux version of the SDK does not include Launcher.

App Engine Launcher

The Windows and OS X versions of the SDK ships with a graphical user interface tool called Launcher that we can use to perform administrative tasks such as creating and managing multiple applications.

Launcher is a very handy tool but bear in mind that while every single task we can accomplish through Launcher can be performed by command-line tools as well, the contrary isn't true. There are tasks that can be performed only from the command line using the proper tools as we will see later in the book.

The following screenshot shows the Launcher window in OS X:

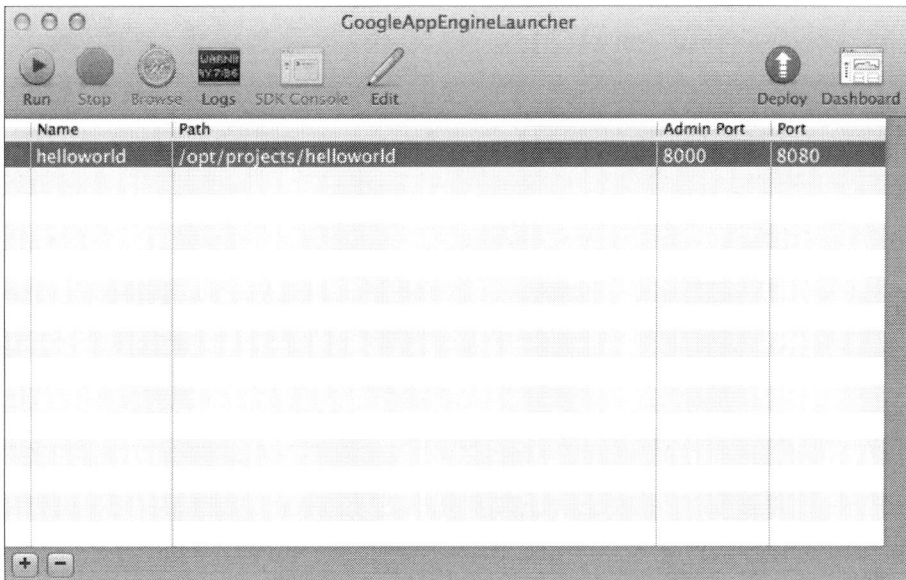

We can see the Launcher in Windows in the following screenshot:

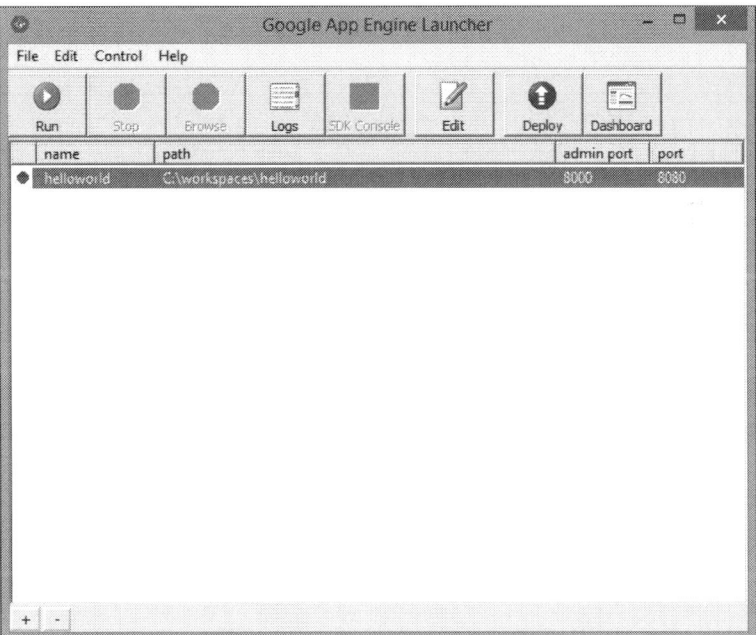

Getting Started

Before we start using the Launcher it's important to check whether it is using the right Python version. This is very important if we have more than one Python installation in our system. To check the Python version used by Launcher and to change it, we can open the **Preferences...** dialog by clicking the appropriate menu depending on our platform and set the Python path value. In the same dialog we can specify which text editor Launcher will open by default when we need to edit application files.

To create a new application we can click **New Application** in the **File** menu or click the button with a plus sign icon in the bottom-left corner of the Launcher window. Launcher will prompt for the application name and the path to the folder that will contain all the project files; once created, the application will be listed in the main window of Launcher.

We can start the local development server by clicking the **Run** button on the Launcher toolbar or clicking **Run** in the **Control** menu. Once the server is started, we can stop it by clicking on the **Stop** button or the **Stop** entry in the **Control** menu. Clicking the **Browse** button or the **Browse** entry in the **Control** menu opens the default browser at the home page of the selected application. To browse the logs produced by the development server, we can open the **Log Console** window by clicking the **Logs** button on the toolbar or the **Logs** entry in the **Control** menu. The **SDK Console** button on the toolbar and the **SDK Console** action on the **Control** menu will open the default browser at the URL that serves the Developer Console, a built-in application to interact with the local development server, which we will explore in detail later in this chapter.

The **Edit** button will open the configuration file for the selected application in an external text editor, maybe the one we specified in the **Preferences...** dialog; the same happens when we click the **Open in External Editor** action in the **Edit** menu.

To deploy and upload the selected application to App Engine we can click the **Deploy** button on the toolbar or click the **Deploy** action in the **Control** menu. The **Dashboard** button on the toolbar and the **Dashboard** action in the **Control** menu will open the default browser at the URL of App Engine Administrative Console.

Using Launcher we can set additional flags for the local development server and customize some parameters such as the TCP port number to which listens. To do so we have to click the **Application Settings...** entry in the **Edit** menu and make the desired adjustments in the settings dialog.

Launcher can also handle existing applications created from scratch through the command line or checked out from an external repository. To add an existing application to the Launcher, we can click the **Add Existing Application...** entry in the **File** menu and specify the application path.

Creating the application

The first step to create an application is pick a name for it. According to the tradition we're going to write an application that will print **"Hello, World!"** so we can choose `helloword` as the application name. We already know how to create an application from Launcher, the alternative is to do it manually from the command line.

At the simplest, a working Python application consists of a folder called application root that contains an `app.yaml` configuration file and a Python module with the code needed to handle HTTP requests. When we create an application within Launcher, it takes care of generating those files and the `root` folder for us, but let's see how can we can accomplish the same result from the command line.

The app.yaml configuration file

When we start creating the `root` folder, it doesn't matter how we name it but to be consistent with Launcher we can use the application's name:

`mkdir helloworld && cd helloworld`

We then create an `app.yaml` file that contains the following YAML code:

```
application: helloworld
version: 1
runtime: python27
api_version: 1
threadsafe: yes

handlers:
- url: .*
  script: main.app

libraries:
- name: webapp2
  version: "2.5.2"
```

> **YAML (a recursive acronym for YAML Ain't Markup Language)** is a human-readable serialization format that is suitable for configuration files that have to be accessed and manipulated both from users and programmatically.

[19]

The first section of the previous code defines some setup parameters for
the application:

- **The `application` parameter**: This is the application name; later in the
  chapter, we'll see how important it is.
- **The `version` parameter**: This is a string that specifies the version of the
  application. App Engine retains a copy of each version deployed and we
  can run them selectively, a very useful feature for testing an application
  before making it public.
- **The `runtime` parameter**: At the time of writing this book, Python 27 is the
  only runtime available for newly created applications as Python 25 was
  deprecated.
- **The `api_version` parameter**: This is the version of the API for the current
  runtime environment. At the time writing this, 1 is the only API version
  available for the Python 27 runtime.
- **The `threadsafe` parameter**: This specifies whether our application can
  handle requests concurrently in separate threads or not.

The next section of the `app.yaml` file lists the URLs we want to match in the form
of a regular expression; the `script` property specifies the handler for each URL.
A handler is a procedure App Engine invokes to provide a response when an
application receives a request. There are two types of handlers:

- **The `script` handlers**: These handlers run the Python code provided by
  the application
- **The `static file` handlers**: These handlers return the content of a static
  resource such as an image or a file that contain the JavaScript code

In this case, we are using a `script` handler, a Python callable addressed with a dot
notation import string: App Engine will match any URL and invoke the `app` object
contained in the `main` module.

The final section lists the name and version of third-party modules provided by App
Engine we want to use from our application, and in this case we only need the latest
version of the webapp2 web framework. We might wonder why we need something
complex such as a web framework to simply print a **"Hello, World!"** message, but as
we already know, our handler must implement a WSGI-compliant interface and this
is exactly one of the features provided by webapp2. We will see how to use it in the
next section.

The main.py application script

Now that the application is configured, we need to provide logic, so we create a file named `main.py` in the application root folder that will contain the following:

```
import webapp2

class MainHandler(webapp2.RequestHandler):
    def get(self):
        self.response.write('Hello world!')

app = webapp2.WSGIApplication([
    ('/', MainHandler)
], debug=True)
```

In the first line of the previous code we import the `webapp2` package into our code, and then we proceed to define a class named `MainHandler` that is derived from the `RequestHandler` class provided by the framework. The base class implements a behavior that makes it very easy to implement a handler for HTTP requests; all we have to do is to define a method named after the HTTP action we want to handle. In this case, we implement the `get()` method that will be automatically invoked whenever the application receives a request of the type GET. The `RequestHandler` class also provides a `self.response` property we can use to access the response object that will be returned to the application server. This property is a file-like object that supports a `write()` method we can use to add content to the body of the HTTP response; in this case we write a string inside the response body with the default content type `text/html` so that it will be shown inside the browser.

Right after the `MainHandler` class definition we create the `app` object, which is an instance of the `WSGIApplication` class provided by webapp2 that implements the WSGI-compliant callable entry point we specified in `app.yaml` with the import string `main.app`. We pass two parameters to the class constructor, a list of URL patterns, and a Boolean flag stating whether the application should run in debug mode or not. URL patterns are tuples that contain two elements: a regular expression that matches requested URLs and a class object derived from `webapp2.RequestHandler` class that will be instantiated to handle requests. URL patterns are processed one by one in the order they are in the list until one matches and the corresponding handler is called.

As we may notice, URL mappings take place twice—firstly in the `app.yaml` file, where a URL is routed to a WSGI compatible application in our code and then in the `WSGIApplication` class instance, where an URL is routed to a request handler object. We can freely choose how to use these mappings, that is either route all URLs in the `app.yaml` file to a single webapp2 application where they are dispatched to handlers or to different URLs to different, smaller webapp2 applications.

Running the development server

The App Engine SDK provides an extremely useful tool called **development server** that runs on our local system emulating the runtime environment we will find in production. This way, we can test our applications locally as we write them. We already know how to start the development server from Launcher. To launch it from the command line instead, we run the `dev_appserver.py` command tool passing the root folder of the application we want to execute as an argument. For example, if we're already inside the root folder of our `helloworld` application, to start the server, we can run this command:

`dev_appserver.py .`

The development server will print some status information on the shell and will then start listen at the local host to the default TCP ports 8000 and 8080, serving the admin console and the application respectively.

While the server is running, we can open a browser, point it at `http://localhost:8080` and see our first web application serving content.

The following screenshot shows the output:

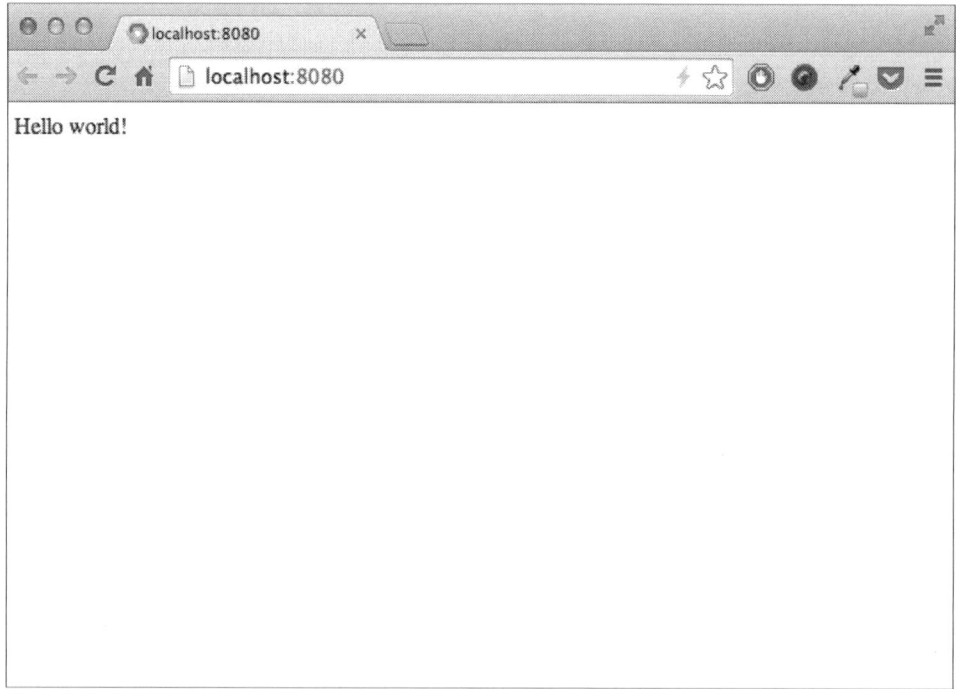

If we are using Launcher, we can simply press the **Browse** button and the browser will be opened automatically at the right URL.

The development server automatically restarts application instances whenever it detects that some content on the application root folder has changed. For example, while the server is running we can try to change the Python code that alters the string we write in the response body:

```
import webapp2

class MainHandler(webapp2.RequestHandler):
    def get(self):
        self.response.write('<H1>Hello world!</H1>')
        self.response.write("<p>I'm using App Engine!</p>")

app = webapp2.WSGIApplication([
    ('/', MainHandler)
], debug=True)
```

After saving the file, we can refresh the browser and immediately see the changes without reloading the server, as shown in the following screenshot:

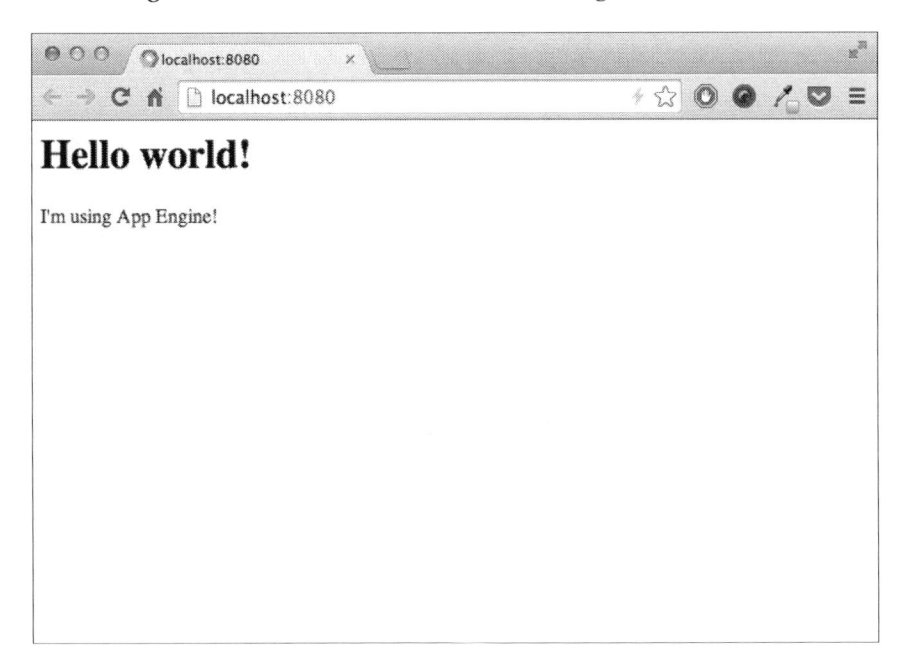

We can now move our application to a production server on App Engine and make it available through the Internet.

Uploading the application to App Engine

Every application running on App Engine is uniquely identified by its name within the Google Cloud Platform. That is why sometimes we find parts of the documentation and tools referring to that as application ID. When working on a local system, we can safely pick any name we want for an application as the local server does not enforce any control on the application ID; but, if we want to deploy an application in production, the application ID must be validated and registered through App Engine Admin Console.

Admin Console can be accessed at `https://appengine.google.com/` and log in with a valid Google user account or a Google apps account for custom domains. If we are using Application Launcher, clicking the **Dashboard** button will open the browser at the right address for us. Once logged in, we can click the **Create Application** button to access the application creation page. We have to provide an application ID (the console will tell us whether it is valid and available) and a title for the application and we're done. For now, we can accept the default values for the remaining options; clicking on **Create Application** again will finally register the application's ID for us.

Now we have to change the dummy application ID we provided for our application with the one registered on App Engine. Open the `app.yaml` configuration file and change the `application` property accordingly:

```
application: the_registered_application_ID
version: 1
runtime: python27
api_version: 1
threadsafe: yes

handlers:
- url: .*
  script: main.app

libraries:
- name: webapp2
  version: "2.5.2"
```

We are now ready to deploy the application on App Engine. If we are using Application Launcher, all we have to do is click on the **Deploy** button in the toolbar. Launcher will ask for our Google credentials and then the log window will open showing the deployment status. If everything went fine the last line shown should be something like this:

```
*** appcfg.py has finished with exit code 0 ***
```

Deploying from the command line is just as easy; from the application root directory, we issue the command:

```
appcfg.py update .
```

We will be prompted for our Google account credentials, and then the deployment will proceed automatically.

Every App Engine application running in production can be accessed via `http://the_registered_application_ID.appspot.com/`, so we can tell whether the application is actually working by accessing this URL from a browser and checking whether the output is the same as that produced by the local development server.

Google App Engine allow us to serve content over **HTTPS (HTTP Secure)** connections on top of the **Secure Sockets Layer** (**SSL**) protocol, which means that data transferred from and to the server is encrypted. When using the `appspot.com` domain, this option is free of charge. To enable secure connections between clients and the App Engine server, all we have to do is add the `secure` option to the URLs listed in the `app.yaml` file:

```
handlers:
- url: .*
  script: main.app
  secure: always
```

On the local development server we will still use regular HTTP connections, but in production we will access `https://the_registered_application_ID.appspot.com/` in a secure manner over HTTPS connections.

If we want to access the application over HTTPS through a custom domain instead, such as `example.com`, we have to configure App Engine so that the platform can use our certificates by following the instructions at `https://cloud.google.com/appengine/docs/ssl`. This service has a fee and we will be charged monthly.

Google Developer Console

Before Google Cloud Platform was released, Admin Console was the only tool available to developers to perform administrative and monitoring tasks on App Engine applications. Admin Console provides a lot of functionalities and it's still powerful enough to manage App Engine applications of any size. However, it's not the right tool if we extensively use the new range of services offered by the Google Cloud Platform, especially if we store data on Google Cloud Storage or our database server is Google Cloud SQL; in this case, to collect information such as billing data and usage history we have to interact with other tools.

Recently Google released **Developer Console**, a comprehensive tool to manage and monitor services, resources, authentication, and billing information for Google Cloud Platform, including App Engine applications. We can access the Developer Console at https://console.developers.google.com/ and log in with a valid Google user account or a Google apps account for custom domains.

To emphasize the concept that developers can combine various pieces coming from Google's cloud infrastructure to build complex applications, Developer Console introduces the notion of cloud projects. A project is a set of functionally grouped cloud products that share the same team and billing information. At the core of a project there is always an App Engine application: every time we create a project, an App Engine application pops up in Admin Console. Simultaneously, when we register an application in Admin Console, a corresponding project is created and listed in Developer Console. Every project is identified by a descriptive name, which is a unique identifier called project ID that is also the ID of the related App Engine application and another unique identifier that is automatically generated called project number.

Beside creating and deleting projects, the developer console also let us do the following:

- **Manage project members**: When we create a project we become the owner of that project. As owners, we can add or remove members and set their permissions.
- **Manage APIs**: We can add or remove API services provided by Google Cloud Platform, set up billing, and monitor data.
- **Manage applications identity**: We can tie requests to specific projects so that we can monitor specific traffic and billing and enforce quotas if needed.
- **Manage applications security**: We can set up OAuth2 for our applications or provide API keys to authorize requests.
- **Filter and cap services**: We can allow requests coming only from authorized hosts or IP addresses and limit the amount of requests allowed for each user every second or every day for all the users.

For every service of Google Cloud Platform, Developer Console provides us with handy tools to perform maintenance operations through the web interface. For example, we can add or remove Google Cloud SQL instances, perform queries on Google Cloud Datastore, browse and manipulate the content of Google Cloud Storage, and manage virtual machines running on Google Compute Engine. We will use several parts of Developer Console later in the book.

Development Console

When we are on the local development server we can still access a tool to browse and manage Datastore, task queues, cron jobs, and other App Engine emulated components running locally. This tool is called **Development Console** and is accessible at `http://localhost:8000` when the local server is active.

Summary

In this chapter we have learned what Google Cloud Platform is, the tools and services it provides, and how we can use them to develop and run fast and scalable web applications written in Python.

We explored what tools we need to start developing with Python for the App Engine platform, how to run an application locally with the development server, and how fast and easy it is to upload it in a production server, ready to be served through the Internet.

The simple example we used in the chapter, although a fully functional App Engine application, is quite simple and it doesn't make use of anything provided by the platform besides the runtime environment. In the next chapter, we will start from scratch with a new, more useful application, exploring the webapp2 framework and taking advantage of Cloud Datastore.

2
A More Complex Application

Web applications commonly provide a set of features such as user authentication and data storage. As we know from the previous chapter, App Engine provides the services and tools needed to implement such features and the best way to learn how to use them is by writing a web application and seeing the platform in action.

In this chapter, we will cover the following topics:

- Further details of the webapp2 framework
- How to authenticate users
- Storing data on Google Cloud Datastore
- Building HTML pages using templates
- Serving static files

Experimenting on the Notes application

To better explore App Engine and Cloud Platform capabilities, we need a real-world application to experiment on; something that's not trivial to write, with a reasonable list of requirements so that it can fit in this book. A good candidate is a note-taking application; we will name it Notes.

Notes enable the users to add, remove, and modify a list of notes; a note has a title and a body of text. Users can only see their personal notes, so they must authenticate before using the application.

The main page of the application will show the list of notes for logged-in users and a form to add new ones.

A More Complex Application

The code from the `helloworld` example in the previous chapter is a good starting point. We can simply change the name of the root folder and the `application` field in the `app.yaml` file to match the new name we chose for the application, or we can start a new project from scratch named `notes`.

Authenticating users

The first requirement for our Notes application is showing the home page only to users who are logged in and redirect others to the login form; the **users** service provided by App Engine is exactly what we need and adding it to our `MainHandler` class is quite simple:

```
import webapp2

from google.appengine.api import users

class MainHandler(webapp2.RequestHandler):
    def get(self):
        user = users.get_current_user()
        if user is not None:
            self.response.write('Hello Notes!')
        else:
            login_url = users.create_login_url(self.request.uri)
            self.redirect(login_url)
app = webapp2.WSGIApplication([
    ('/', MainHandler)
], debug=True)
```

The `user` package we import on the second line of the previous code provides access to users' service functionalities. Inside the `get()` method of the `MainHandler` class, we first check whether the user visiting the page has logged in or not. If they have, the `get_current_user()` method returns an instance of the `user` class provided by App Engine and representing an authenticated user; otherwise, it returns `None` as output. If the user is valid, we provide the response as we did before; otherwise, we redirect them to the Google login form. The URL of the login form is returned using the `create_login_url()` method, and we call it, passing as a parameter the URL we want to redirect users to after a successful authentication. In this case, we want to redirect users to the same URL they are visiting, provided by webapp2 in the `self.request.uri` property. The webapp2 framework also provides handlers with a `redirect()` method we can use to conveniently set the right status and location properties of the response object so that the client browsers will be redirected to the login page.

HTML templates with Jinja2

Web applications provide rich and complex HTML user interfaces, and Notes is no exception but, so far, response objects in our applications contained just small pieces of text. We could include HTML tags as strings in our Python modules and write them in the response body but we can imagine how easily it could become messy and hard to maintain the code. We need to completely separate the Python code from HTML pages and that's exactly what a template engine does. A template is a piece of HTML code living in its own file and possibly containing additional, special tags; with the help of a template engine, from the Python script, we can load this file, properly parse special tags, if any, and return valid HTML code in the response body. App Engine includes in the Python runtime a well-known template engine: the Jinja2 library.

To make the Jinja2 library available to our application, we need to add this code to the `app.yaml` file under the `libraries` section:

```
libraries:
- name: webapp2
  version: "2.5.2"
- name: jinja2
  version: latest
```

We can put the HTML code for the main page in a file called `main.html` inside the application root. We start with a very simple page:

```
<!DOCTYPE html>
<html>
<head lang="en">
  <meta charset="UTF-8">
  <title>Notes</title>
</head>
<body>
  <div class="container">

    <h1>Welcome to Notes!</h1>

    <p>
      Hello, <b>{{user}}</b> - <a href="{{logout_url}}">Logout</a>
    </p>

  </div>
</body>
</html>
```

A More Complex Application

Most of the content is static, which means that it will be rendered as standard HTML as we see it but there is a part that is dynamic and whose content depend on which data will be passed at runtime to the rendering process. This data is commonly referred to as **template context**.

What has to be dynamic is the username of the current user and the link used to log out from the application. The HTML code contains two special elements written in the Jinja2 template syntax, `{{user}}` and `{{logout_url}}`, that will be substituted before the final output occurs.

Back to the Python script; we need to add the code to initialize the template engine before the `MainHandler` class definition:

```python
import os
import jinja2

jinja_env = jinja2.Environment(
    loader=jinja2.FileSystemLoader(os.path.dirname(__file__)))
```

The environment instance stores engine configuration and global objects, and it's used to load templates instances; in our case, instances are loaded from HTML files on the filesystem in the same directory as the Python script.

To load and render our template, we add the following code to the `MainHandler.get()` method:

```python
class MainHandler(webapp2.RequestHandler):
    def get(self):
        user = users.get_current_user()
        if user is not None:
            logout_url = users.create_logout_url(self.request.uri)
            template_context = {
                'user': user.nickname(),
                'logout_url': logout_url,
            }
            template = jinja_env.get_template('main.html')
            self.response.out.write(
                template.render(template_context))
        else:
            login_url = users.create_login_url(self.request.uri)
            self.redirect(login_url)
```

Similar to how we get the login URL, the `create_logout_url()` method provided by the user service returns the absolute URI to the logout procedure that we assign to the `logout_url` variable.

We then create the `template_context` dictionary that contains the context values we want to pass to the template engine for the rendering process. We assign the nickname of the current user to the `user` key in the dictionary and the logout URL string to the `logout_url` key.

The `get_template()` method from the `jinja_env` instance takes the name of the file that contains the HTML code and returns a Jinja2 template object. To obtain the final output, we call the `render()` method on the `template` object passing in the `template_context` dictionary whose values will be accessed, specifying their respective keys in the HTML file with the template syntax elements `{{user}}` and `{{logout_url}}`.

This is the result of the template rendering:

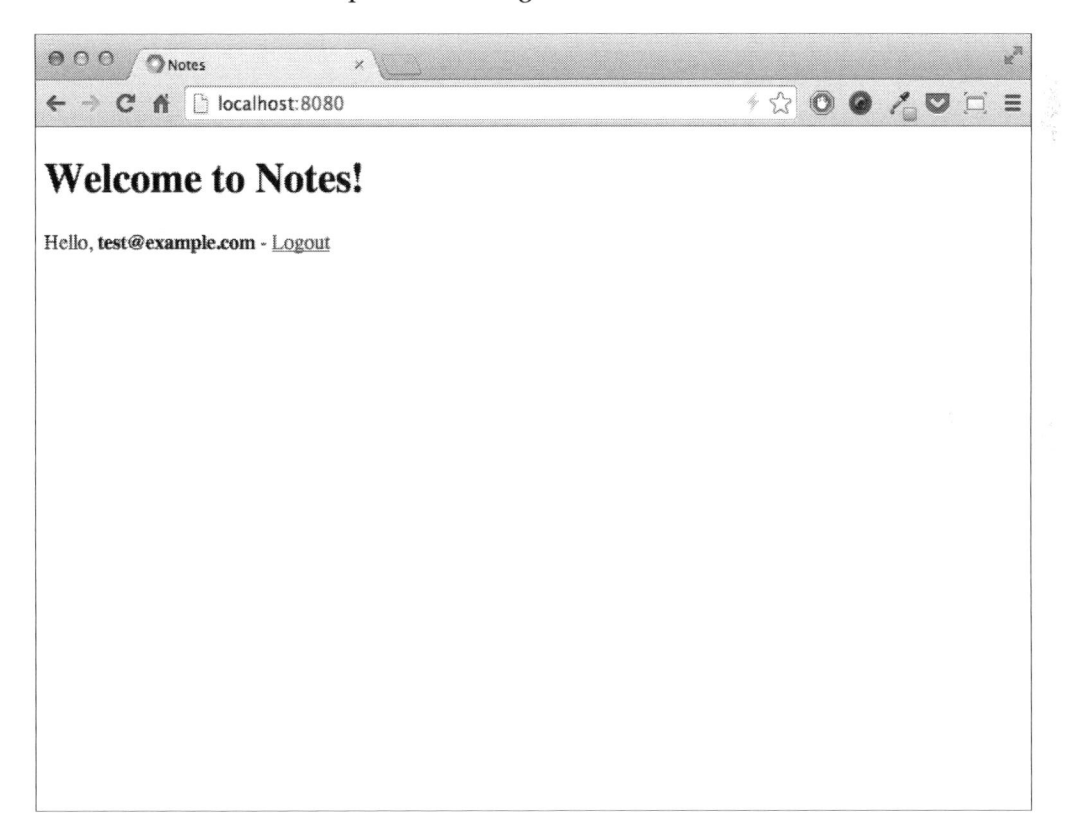

Handling forms

The main page of the application is supposed to list all the notes that belong to the current user but there isn't any way to create such notes at the moment. We need to display a web form on the main page so that users can submit details and create a note.

To display a form to collect data and create notes, we put the following HTML code right below the username and the logout link in the `main.html` template file:

```
{% if note_title %}
<p>Title: {{note_title}}</p>
<p>Content: {{note_content}}</p>
{% endif %}

<h4>Add a new note</h4>
<form action="" method="post">
  <div class="form-group">
    <label for="title">Title:</label>
    <input type="text" id="title" name="title" />
  </div>
  <div class="form-group">
      <label for="content">Content:</label>
      <textarea id="content" name="content"></textarea>
  </div>
  <div class="form-group">
      <button type="submit">Save note</button>
  </div>
</form>
```

Before showing the form, a message is displayed only when the template context contains a variable named `note_title`. To do this, we use an `if` statement, executed between the `{% if note_title %}` and `{% endif %}` delimiters; similar delimiters are used to perform `for` loops or assign values inside a template.

The `action` property of the `form` tag is empty; this means that upon form submission, the browser will perform a POST request to the same URL, which in this case is the home page URL. As our WSGI application maps the home page to the `MainHandler` class, we need to add a method to this class so that it can handle POST requests:

```
class MainHandler(webapp2.RequestHandler):
    def get(self):
        user = users.get_current_user()
```

```
            if user is not None:
                logout_url = users.create_logout_url(self.request.uri)
                template_context = {
                    'user': user.nickname(),
                    'logout_url': logout_url,
                }
                template = jinja_env.get_template('main.html')
                self.response.out.write(
                    template.render(template_context))
            else:
                login_url = users.create_login_url(self.request.uri)
                self.redirect(login_url)

    def post(self):
        user = users.get_current_user()
        if user is None:
            self.error(401)

        logout_url = users.create_logout_url(self.request.uri)
        template_context = {
            'user': user.nickname(),
            'logout_url': logout_url,
            'note_title': self.request.get('title'),
            'note_content': self.request.get('content'),
        }
        template = jinja_env.get_template('main.html')
        self.response.out.write(
            template.render(template_context))
```

When the form is submitted, the handler is invoked and the `post()` method is called. We first check whether a valid user is logged in; if not, we raise an **HTTP 401: Unauthorized** error without serving any content in the response body. Since the HTML template is the same served by the `get()` method, we still need to add the logout URL and the user name to the context. In this case, we also store the data coming from the HTML form in the context. To access the form data, we call the `get()` method on the `self.request` object. The last three lines are boilerplate code to load and render the home page template. We can move this code in a separate method to avoid duplication:

```
    def _render_template(self, template_name, context=None):
        if context is None:
            context = {}
        template = jinja_env.get_template(template_name)
        return template.render(context)
```

In the handler class, we will then use something like this to output the template rendering result:

```
self.response.out.write(
    self._render_template('main.html', template_context))
```

We can try to submit the form and check whether the note title and content are actually displayed above the form.

Persisting data in Datastore

Even if users can log in and submit a note, our application isn't very useful until notes are stored somewhere. Google Cloud Datastore is the perfect place to store our notes. As part of App Engine's infrastructure, it takes care of data distribution and replication, so all we have to do is define store and retrieve our entities using the Python **NDB (Next DB) Datastore API**.

> There are currently two APIs available in the Python runtime to interact with Datastore: the **DB Datastore API**, also known as ext.db, and the NDB Datastore API. Even if both the APIs store exactly the same data in Datastore, in this book, we will only use NDB; it is more recent, provides more features, and its API is slightly more robust.

An entity has one or more properties that in turn have a name and a type; each entity has a unique key that identifies it, and instead of storing different data in different tables as in a relational database, every entity in Datastore is categorized by a kind. In the Python world, a kind is determined by its model class that we need to define in our application.

Defining the models

To represent a kind, Datastore models must derive from the `ndb.Model` class provided by the NDB API. We define our models in a Python module called `models.py` that contains the following code:

```
from google.appengine.ext import ndb

class Note(ndb.Model):
    title = ndb.StringProperty()
    content = ndb.TextProperty(required=True)
    date_created = ndb.DateTimeProperty(auto_now_add=True)
```

The `Note` class has a property named `title` that contains small text (up to 500 characters), another one named `content` that contains text of unlimited length, and a property named `date_created` that contains a date and a time. Entities of this kind must contain at least a value for the `user` and `content` properties, and if not provided, the `date_created` property value will store the date and time at the moment the entity was created. We can now add new entities of the type `Note` class to the Datastore when users submit the form in the main page of the Notes application. In the `main.py` module, we first need to import the `Note` class from the `models` module:

```
from models import Note
```

Then, we modify the `post()` method as follows:

```
def post(self):
    user = users.get_current_user()
    if user is None:
        self.error(401)

    note = Note(title=self.request.get('title'),
                content=self.request.get('content'))
    note.put()

    logout_url = users.create_logout_url(self.request.uri)
    template_context = {
        'user': user.nickname(),
        'logout_url': logout_url,
    }
    self.response.out.write(
        self._render_template('main.html', template_context))
```

From now on, each time a user submits the form in the main page, an instance of the `Note` class is created and an entity is persisted in the Datastore right after the `put()` method is called. As we have not modified the `template_context` dictionary, the storing process won't do anything apparently. To verify that data is actually stored, we can use the local Development Console by opening the browser at `http://localhost:8000` and checking out Datastore Viewer.

Basic querying

An entity can optionally specify another entity as its **parent** and an entity without a parent is a **root entity**; entities in Datastore form a hierarchically structured space similar to the directory structure in a filesystem. An entity together with all its descendants form an **entity group** and the key of the common ancestor is defined as the **parent key**.

It's important to understand entities' relationship because of the intrinsic distributed nature of the Datastore. Without digging too much into the details, what we have to know is that queries across multiple entity groups cannot guarantee consistent results and the result of such queries can sometimes fail to reflect recent changes to the data.

We have an alternative though; to get strongly consistent results, we can perform a so-called **ancestor query**, which is a query that limits the results to a particular entity group. To use ancestor queries in our code, the first thing to do is add a parent to our note entities when we create the model instance:

```
note = Note(parent=ndb.Key("User", user.nickname()),
            title=self.request.get('title'),
            content=self.request.get('content'))
note.put()
```

As every note belongs to the user who creates it, we can use the same logic to structure our data; we use the currently logged-in user as the parent key for an entity group that contains all the notes belonging to that user. This is why we specify the `parent` keyword when calling the `Note` constructor in the previous code. To obtain the key of the currently logged-in user, we use the `ndb.Key` class constructor, passing in the kind and the identifier of the corresponding entity.

What we need to do now is retrieve our notes from Datastore and show them to our users. As we will use ancestor queries, before proceeding, we add a utility method to the `Note` model class:

```
class Note(ndb.Model):
    title = ndb.StringProperty()
    content = ndb.TextProperty(required=True)
    date_created = ndb.DateTimeProperty(auto_now_add=True)

    @classmethod
    def owner_query(cls, parent_key):
        return cls.query(ancestor=parent_key).order(
            -cls.date_created)
```

The `owner_query()` method returns a query object already filtered and containing the group entities for the parent key specified with the `parent_key` function parameter.

To load all notes belonging to the current user, we then write the following:

```
user = users.get_current_user()
ancestor_key = ndb.Key("User", user.nickname())
qry = Note.owner_query(ancestor_key)
notes = qry.fetch()
```

As we want to show the notes in the main page in the case of the GET and POST requests, we can load the entities inside the `_render_template()` method, which is called by the handler in both cases:

```
def _render_template(self, template_name, context=None):
    if context is None:
        context = {}

    user = users.get_current_user()
    ancestor_key = ndb.Key("User", user.nickname())
    qry = Note.owner_query(ancestor_key)
    context['notes'] = qry.fetch()

    template = jinja_env.get_template(template_name)
    return template.render(context)
```

We add the list of the notes as a value for the `notes` key in the `context` dictionary so that we can use them in the HTML template by writing the following right below the form:

```
{% for note in notes %}
<div class="note">
  <h4>{{ note.title }}</h4>
  <p class="note-content">{{ note.content }}</p>
</div>
{% endfor %}
```

A `div` element will be printed out for each note in the query result and nothing will be printed out if the query returned an empty list. Even if the `title` property is optional for entities of the kind Note, we can safely access it. If it's not present, an empty string will be returned.

Transactions

It's very common for web applications to define and use Datastore models that depend on each other so that when we update an entity, we will likely need to update dependent entities as well. However, what happens if, during a series of Datastore operations, some of them fail? In such cases, we can encapsulate these operations in a transaction so that either all of them succeed or all of them fail.

To see a use case for transactions, we add a small feature to our Note model: a checklist. A checklist is a list of items that provide a Boolean property that determines their checked state. We first need to define a Datastore model for a single checklist item:

```python
class CheckListItem(ndb.Model):
    title = ndb.StringProperty()
    checked = ndb.BooleanProperty(default=False)
```

The entity has two properties, the `title` property for the string that will be displayed and the `checked` property to store whether the item is checked or not.

We then add a property to the `Node` model class referencing item entities:

```python
class Note(ndb.Model):
    title = ndb.StringProperty()
    content = ndb.TextProperty(required=True)
    date_created = ndb.DateTimeProperty(auto_now_add=True)
    checklist_items = ndb.KeyProperty("CheckListItem",
                                       repeated=True)

    @classmethod
    def owner_query(cls, parent_key):
        return cls.query(ancestor=parent_key).order(
            -cls.date_created)
```

The `checklist_items` property stores key values of the `CheckListItem` kind; the `repeated=True` parameter is needed to define that the property can hold more than one value.

Users can create checklist items for a note filling the creation form with a comma-separated list of values, so we add the following to the HTML template:

```html
<form action="" method="post">
  <div class="form-group">
    <label for="title">Title:</label>
```

```
            <input type="text" id="title" name="title"/>
        </div>
        <div class="form-group">
            <label for="content">Content:</label>
            <textarea id="content" name="content"></textarea>
        </div>
        <div class="form-group">
            <label for="checklist_items">Checklist items:</label>
            <input type="text" id="checklist_items" name="checklist_items" placeholder="comma,separated,values"/>
        </div>
        <div class="form-group">
            <button type="submit">Save note</button>
        </div>
    </form>
```

Now, we have to handle the comma-separated list in the `MainHandler` class:

```
note = Note(parent=ndb.Key("User", user.nickname()),
            title=self.request.get('title'),
            content=self.request.get('content'))
note.put()

item_titles = self.request.get('checklist_items').split(',')
for item_title in item_titles:
    item = CheckListItem(parent=note.key, title=item_title)
    item.put()
    note.checklist_items.append(item.key)

note.put()
```

We first retrieve the comma-separated values representing checklist items from the request. Then, for each of them, we create a `CheckListItem` instance. Until a model instance is not persisted, Datastore does not assign any key to it. So, we need to first store each item by calling the `put()` method before accessing the `key` property and retrieving a `Key` instance for that entity. Once we have a valid key, we append it to the list of items of the `Note` instance. We pass the key of the note as parent for the items so that all these entities will be part of the same entity group. The last step is to call the `put()` method and update the Node entity and store the new data for the `checklist_items` property.

A More Complex Application

Now what happens if the `note.put()` method fails? We have a bunch of entities of `CheckListItem` type that are not tied to any note, and this is a consistency problem. Transactions can help us refactor the creation of a note so that it can either succeed or fail, without leaving behind any dangling data. We encapsulate the creation of note objects in a separate `_create_node()` method in the handler class:

```
@ndb.transactional
def _create_note(self, user):
    note = Note(parent=ndb.Key("User", user.nickname()),
                title=self.request.get('title'),
                content=self.request.get('content'))
    note.put()

    item_titles = self.request.get('checklist_items').split(',')
    for item_title in item_titles:
        item = CheckListItem(parent=note.key, title=item_title)
        item.put()
        note.checklist_items.append(item.key)

    note.put()
```

The `@ndb.transactional` decorator is all the Python code we need. Datastore will then ensure that any operation in the decorated method happens within a transaction. In this way, either we create a note entity along with all the checklist items entities or we get an error without touching the underlying data. To complete the code, we have to call the `_create_node()` method inside the `post()` method:

```
def post(self):
    user = users.get_current_user()
    if user is None:
        self.error(401)

    self._create_note(user)

    logout_url = users.create_logout_url(self.request.uri)
    template_context = {
        'user': user.nickname(),
        'logout_url': logout_url,
    }
    self.response.out.write(
        self._render_template('main.html', template_context))
```

To show the list of items in a checklist for our notes, we must add the code needed in the HTML template:

```
{% for note in notes %}
<div class="note">
  <h4>{{ note.title }}</h4>
  <p class="note-content">{{ note.content }}</p>
  {% if note.checklist_items %}
  <ul>
    {% for item in note.checklist_items %}
    <li class="{%if item.get().checked%}checked{%endif%}">{{item.get().title}}</li>
    {% endfor %}
  </ul>
  {% endif %}
</div>
{% endfor %}
```

We add an unordered list if the `checklist_items` property is not empty. We then iterate the list of items, adding a `class` attribute containing the `checked` parameter whenever an item has its `checked` property set to the `true` value: later in this chapter, we'll learn how to add a **CSS (Cascading Style Sheets)** rule so that when this class is present, the item is shown with a horizontal line through its center.

Using static files

Usually web applications make use of CSS and JavaScript resources to provide a better user experience. For efficiency reasons, such content is not dynamically served by the WSGI application and are delivered by App Engine as static files instead.

We know from the previous chapter that App Engine provides two types of handlers, script handlers and static file handlers. We add a static file handler to our `app.yaml` configuration file like this:

```
handlers:
- url: /static
  static_dir: static

- url: .*
  script: main.app
```

A More Complex Application

The syntax is almost the same as for script handlers. We specify a URL to map as a regular expression but instead of providing a Python script to handle requests, we specify a filesystem path relative to the application root where the files and directories that need to be served as static resources are located.

> We are now going to provide a minimal style for our HTML pages by manually coding some CSS rules. While it is acceptable for the scope of the book to get our hands dirty learning how to build a custom design from scratch, in the real world, we might prefer to use frontend frameworks such as Bootstrap (http://getbootstrap.com/) or Foundation (http://foundation.zurb.com/) to easily provide state-of-the-art aesthetics, cross-browser capabilities, and responsive layouts for mobile devices.

To provide a CSS for our application, we then create the `static/css` folder into our application root:

```
mkdir -p static/css
```

This folder should contain a file called `notes.css` that will contain the style sheet for our application:

```css
body {
    font-family: "helvetica", sans-serif;
    background: #e8e8e8;
    color: rgba(39,65,90,.9);
    text-align: center;
}

div.container {
    width: 600px;
    display: inline-block;
}
```

The first part is for global layout elements; we will put the form and the notes one below another in a centered container. We then style the form:

```css
form {
    background: white;
    padding-bottom: 0.5em;
    margin-bottom: 30px;
}
h4,legend {
    margin-bottom: 10px;
    font-size: 21px;
    font-weight: 400;
}
```

The form will be contained in a white box and the legend will look like a note title. Form elements will be styled as follows:

```css
div.form-group {
    margin-bottom: 1em;
}

label {
    display: inline-block;
    width: 120px;
    text-align: right;
    padding-right: 15px;
}

input, textarea {
    width: 250px;
    height: 35px;
    -moz-box-sizing: border-box;
    box-sizing: border-box;
    border: 1px solid #999;
    font-size: 14px;
    border-radius: 4px;
    padding: 6px;
}

textarea {
    vertical-align: top;
    height: 5em;
    resize: vertical;
}
```

We then proceed with styling the white boxes that contain the Notes data:

```css
div.note {
    background: white;
    vertical-align: baseline;
    display: block;
    margin: 0 auto 30px auto;
}

legend, div.note > h4 {
    padding: 18px 0 15px;
    margin: 0 0 10px;
    background: #00a1ff;
    color: white;
}
```

A More Complex Application

The last part of the style sheet is dedicated to notes checklists. We provide a style for unordered lists contained in `div` elements with a `note` class and a style for list items in checked state:

```css
div.note > ul {
    margin: 0;
    padding: 0;
    list-style: none;
    border-top: 2px solid #e7f2f0;
}

div.note > ul > li {
    font-size: 21px;
    padding: 18px 0 18px 18px;
    border-bottom: 2px solid #e7f2f0;
    text-align: left;
}
div.note-content {
    text-align: left;
    padding: 0.5em;
}

.checked {
    text-decoration: line-through;
}
```

To use the style sheet, we add this in our HTML template, inside the `<meta>` tag:

```html
<link rel="stylesheet" type="text/css" href="static/css/notes.css">
```

This is how the application should appear once the style sheet is applied:

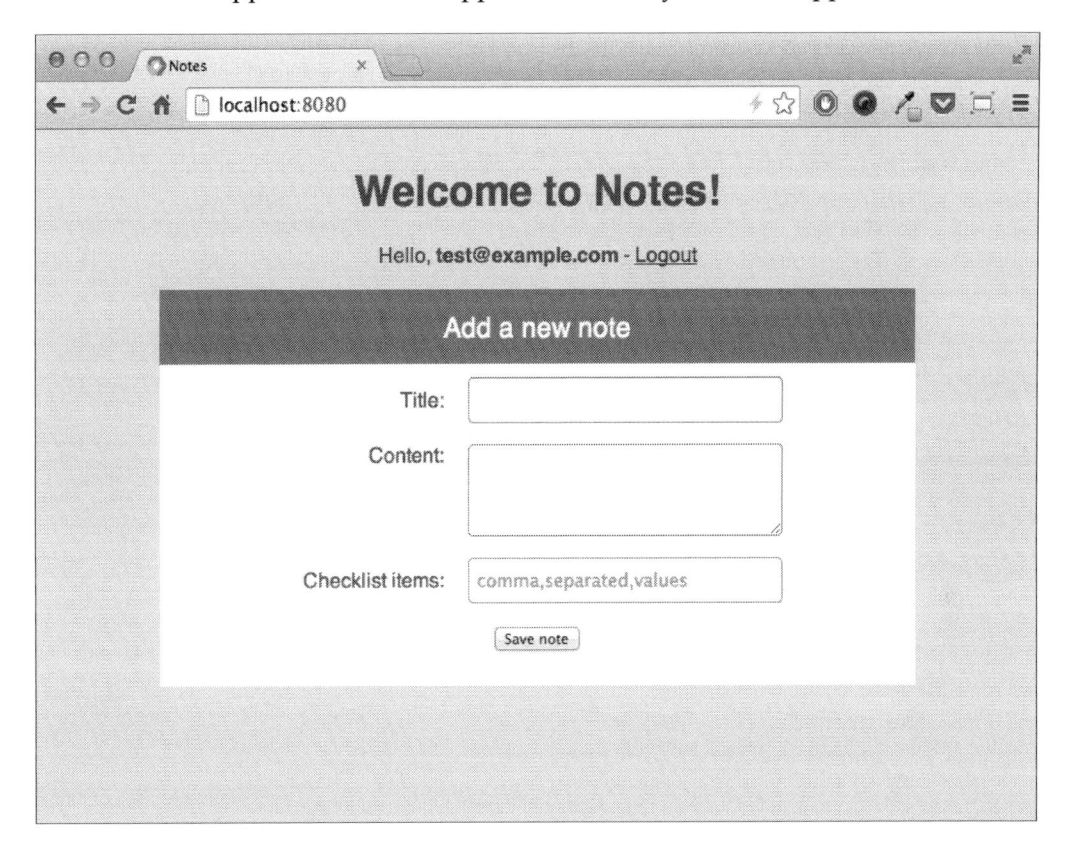

Summary

Thanks to App Engine, we have already implemented a rich set of features with a relatively small effort so far.

In this chapter, we have discovered some more details about the webapp2 framework and its capabilities, implementing a nontrivial request handler. We have learned how to use the App Engine users service to provide users authentication. We have delved into some fundamental details of Datastore and now we know how to structure data in grouped entities and how to effectively retrieve data with ancestor queries. In addition, we have created an HTML user interface with the help of the Jinja2 template library, learning how to serve static content such as CSS files.

In the next chapter, we will keep on adding more and more features to the Notes application, learning how to store uploaded files on Google Cloud Storage, manipulate images, and deal with long operations and scheduled tasks. We will also make the application capable of sending and receiving e-mails.

3
Storing and Processing Users' Data

There are several pieces of data that need to be persisted and that don't fit very well into the Datastore or similar storage systems, such as images and media files in general; these are usually big and their size impacts application costs and how they should be uploaded, stored, and served back when requested. In addition, sometimes we need to modify these contents on the server side and the operation can take a long time.

We will add some features to the Notes application that will raise these kinds of problems, and we will see how App Engine provides everything we need to face them effectively.

In this chapter, we will cover the following topics:

- Adding a form to our application to let users upload images
- Serving the files uploaded back to the clients
- Transforming images with the Images service
- Performing long jobs with the task queue
- Scheduling tasks
- Handling e-mail messages from our application

Uploading files to Google Cloud Storage

It's extremely common for a web application to deal with image files or PDF documents, and Notes is not an exception. It could be very useful for users to attach an image or a document to one or more notes in addition to the title and the description text.

Storing big chunks of binary data in the Datastore would be inefficient and rather expensive, so we need to use a different, dedicated system: Google Cloud Storage. Cloud Storage lets us store large files in locations called **buckets**. An application can read and write from multiple buckets and we can set up an **Access Control List** (**ACL**) to determine who can access a certain bucket and with what permissions. Every App Engine application has its default bucket associated but we can create, manage, and browse any number of them through the Developer Console.

Installing Cloud Storage Client Library

To better interact with Cloud Storage, we need an external piece of software that is not included in the App Engine runtime environment, which is the **GCS Client Library**. This Python library implements functions to easily read and write files inside buckets, handling errors and retries. The following is the detailed list of these functions:

- **The** `open()` **method**: This allows us to operate with a file-like buffer on bucket contents
- **The** `listbucket()` **method**: This retrieves the contents of a bucket
- **The** `stat()` **method**: This gets metadata for a file in a bucket
- **The** `delete()` **method**: This removes files from buckets

To install GCS Client Library, we can use pip:

```
pip install GoogleAppEngineCloudStorageClient -t <app_root>
```

It's important to specify the destination directory for the package with the `-t` option, as it is the only way to install third-party packages that are not provided by App Engine on the production server. When we deploy the application, all content in the application root will be copied on the remote server, including the `cloudstorage` package.

It's also possible to clone the **Subversion** (**SVN**) executable and check out the latest version of the source code, provided that we have the `svn` repository installed on our system:

```
svn checkout http://appengine-gcs-client.googlecode.com/svn/trunk/python gcs-client
```

To check whether the library is working, we can issue the following from the command line and verify that no errors are printed out:

```
python -c"import cloudstorage"
```

> An alternative way to interact with Google Cloud Storage is the **Blobstore API**, bundled with the App Engine Environment. Blobstore was the first App Engine service to provide cheap and effective storage for big files, and it's still available even though Cloud Storage is more recent and more actively developed. Even if we do not store any data in Blobstore, we will use the Blobstore API with Cloud Storage later in this chapter.

Adding a form to upload images

We start adding a field in the HTML form that we use to create notes so that the user can specify a file to upload. Before the submit button, we insert an input tag:

```
<div class="form-group">
  <label for="uploaded_file">Attached file:</label>
  <input type="file" id="uploaded_file" name="uploaded_file">
</div>
```

We will store all the files for every user in the default bucket under a folder named after the user ID; our application is the only way to access that file if we do not alter the default access control list, so we can enforce security and privacy at the application level. In order to access the uploaded file from the webapp2 request object, we need to rewrite the post method for the MainHandler class, but first, we need these import statements at the top of the main.py module:

```
from google.appengine.api import app_identity
import cloudstorage
import mimetypes
```

We will see in a moment where to use these modules; this is the code that will be added to the MainHandler class:

```
def post(self):
    user = users.get_current_user()
    if user is None:
        self.error(401)

    bucket_name = app_identity.get_default_gcs_bucket_name()
    uploaded_file = self.request.POST.get('uploaded_file')
    file_name = getattr(uploaded_file, 'filename', None)
```

```python
        file_content = getattr(uploaded_file, 'file', None)
    real_path = ''
    if file_name and file_content:
        content_t = mimetypes.guess_type(file_name)[0]
        real_path = os.path.join('/', bucket_name, user.user_id(),
                                 file_name)

        with cloudstorage.open(real_path, 'w',
                               content_type=content_t) as f:
            f.write(file_content.read())

    self._create_note(user, file_name)

    logout_url = users.create_logout_url(self.request.uri)
    template_context = {
        'user': user.nickname(),
        'logout_url': logout_url,
    }
    self.response.out.write(
        self._render_template('main.html', template_context))
```

We first retrieve the name of the default bucket for our application through the `app_identity` service by calling its `get_default_gcs_bucket_name()` method. Then, we access the `request` object to get the value of the `uploaded_file` field. When users specify a file to upload, `self.request.POST.get('uploaded_file')` returns an instance of the `FileStorage` class defined in the `cgi` module of the Python standard library. The `FieldStorage` object has two fields, `filename` and `file`, that contain the name and the content of the uploaded file, respectively. If users don't specify a file to be uploaded, the value of the `uploaded_file` field becomes an empty string.

When dealing with an uploaded file, we try to guess its type with the help of the `mimetypes` module from the Python standard library, and then we build the full path of the file according to the `/<bucket_name>/<user_id>/<filename>` scheme. The last part involves the GCS Client Library; in fact, it lets us open a file for writing on Cloud Storage as we would do on a regular filesystem. We write the content of the uploaded file by calling the `read` method on the `file_name` object. We finally call the `_create_note` method, passing the name of the file as well, so it will be stored inside a `Note` instance.

> If users upload a file with the same name as another file that's already present in Cloud Storage, the latter will be overwritten with the new data. If we want to handle this issue, some logic should be added, such as either renaming the new file or asking users how to proceed.

Before refactoring the `_create_note()` method to accept and handle the name of the file attached to a note, we need to add a property to our `Note` model class to store the name of the files attached. The model becomes as follows:

```
class Note(ndb.Model):
    title = ndb.StringProperty()
    content = ndb.TextProperty(required=True)
    date_created = ndb.DateTimeProperty(auto_now_add=True)
    checklist_items = ndb.KeyProperty("CheckListItem",
                                      repeated=True)
    files = ndb.StringProperty(repeated=True)

    @classmethod
    def owner_query(cls, parent_key):
        return cls.query(ancestor=parent_key).order(
            -cls.date_created)
```

Even if we only support the addition of a single file during the note creation, we store a list of filenames so that we already provide support for multiple attachments in a single note.

Back in the `main.py` module, we refactor the `_create_note()` method as follows:

```
@ndb.transactional
def _create_note(self, user, file_name):
    note = Note(parent=ndb.Key("User", user.nickname()),
                title=self.request.get('title'),
                content=self.request.get('content'))
    note.put()

    item_titles = self.request.get('checklist_items').split(',')
    for item_title in item_titles:
        item = CheckListItem(parent=note.key, title=item_title)
        item.put()
        note.checklist_items.append(item.key)

    if file_name:
        note.files.append(file_name)

    note.put()
```

When the `file_name` parameter is not set to the `None` value, we add the name of the file and update the `Note` entity. We can now run the code and try to upload a file when creating a note. The code we wrote so far only stores the uploaded file without any feedback, so to check whether everything is working, we need to use the Blobstore viewer on the local Development Console. If we're running the application on production servers, we can use the Cloud Storage interface on Google Developer Console to list the contents of the default bucket.

> At the time of writing this, the local development server emulates Cloud Storage in the very same way as it emulates Blobstore, and this is why we will only find a Blobstore viewer in the Development Console.

Serving files from Cloud Storage

As we didn't specify an Access Control List for the default bucket, it is only accessible from the Developer Console upon authentication or through the Notes application. This is fine as long as we want to keep files private to the user who performed the upload but we need to provide a URL for our application where these files can be retrieved. For example, if a user wants to retrieve the file named `example.png`, the URL could be `/media/example.png`. We need to provide a request handler for such URLs, checking whether the currently logged-in user has uploaded the requested file or not and provide a response accordingly. In the `main.py` module, we add the following class:

```
class MediaHandler(webapp2.RequestHandler):
    def get(self, file_name):
        user = users.get_current_user()
        bucket_name = app_identity.get_default_gcs_bucket_name()
        content_t = mimetypes.guess_type(file_name)[0]
        real_path = os.path.join('/', bucket_name, user.user_id(),
                                 file_name)

        try:
            with cloudstorage.open(real_path, 'r') as f:
                self.response.headers.add_header('Content-Type',
                                                 content_t)
                self.response.out.write(f.read())
        except cloudstorage.errors.NotFoundError:
            self.abort(404)
```

After determining the currently logged-in user, we build the full path to the requested file using the same scheme we used to store the /<bucket_name>/<user_id>/<filename> file. If the file does not exist, GCS Client Library raises a `NotFoundError` error and we serve a **404: Not Found** courtesy page using the `abort()` method of the request handler. If the file is actually in Cloud Storage, we open it to read with the usual file-like interface provided by GCS Client Library, and we write its content in the response body after setting the right `Content-Type` HTTP header. This way, we cannot access any file uploaded by other users even if we know the name of the file, because our user ID will be used to determine the full path of the file.

To use the `MediaHandler` class, we add a tuple to the `WSGIApplication` constructor:

```
app = webapp2.WSGIApplication([
    (r'/', MainHandler),
    (r'/media/(?P<file_name>[\w.]{0,256})', MediaHandler),
], debug=True)
```

The regular expression tries to match any URL that starts with the /media/ path followed by a filename. When matching, the regular expression group named `file_name` is passed to the `get()` method of the `MediaHandler` class as a parameter.

The last step is to add a link for each file attached to a note in the main page so that users can download them. We simply add a `for` iteration on the `main.html` template right before the iteration of the checklist items:

```
{% if note.files %}
<ul>
  {% for file in note.files %}
  <li class="file"><a href="/media/{{ file }}">{{ file }}</a></li>
  {% endfor %}
</ul>
{% endif %}
```

We finally add the CSS `file` class to `li` elements to distinguish files from checklist items; we add the corresponding styles to the `note.css` file:

```
div.note > ul > li.file {
    border: 0;
    background: #0070B3;
}

li.file > a {
    color: white;
    text-decoration: none;
}
```

With this updated style sheet, the background for file items has a different color from checklist items and the link text color is white.

Serving files through Google's Content Delivery Network

We are currently serving files attached to the notes with our WSGI application through the `MediaHandler` request handler class, and this is very convenient because we can perform security checks and ensure that users only get files they have previously updated. This approach has several drawbacks, though: the application is less efficient compared to a regular web server and we consume resources such as memory and bandwidth, which could potentially cost us a lot of money.

There is an alternative, however; if we relax the requirements for our Notes application and allow the contents to be publicly available, we can deliver such files with low latency from a highly optimized and cookie-less infrastructure: the **Google Content Delivery Network (CDN)**. How to do this depends on which kind of files we have to deliver: images or any other **MIME** type.

Serving images

If we are dealing with an image file, we can use the Images service to generate a URL, which is public but not guessable, to reach content stored in Cloud Storage. First, we need to compute an encoded key representing the file in Cloud Storage that we want to serve; to do this, we use the `create_gs_key()` method provided by the Blobstore API. We then use the `get_serving_url()` method provided by the Images service to generate a serving URL for the encoded key. If we need to serve the same image with different sizes—for example, to provide a thumbnail—there is no need to store the same file multiple times; in fact, we can specify a size for the image we want to deliver and the CDN will take care of it. We need to import the packages needed at the top of the `main.py` module:

```
from google.appengine.api import images
from google.appengine.ext import blobstore
```

For convenience, we add a `_get_urls_for()` method to the `MainHandler` class we can call whenever we want to get serving URLs for a file in Cloud Storage:

```
def _get_urls_for(self, file_name):
    user = users.get_current_user()
    if user is None:
        return

    bucket_name = app_identity.get_default_gcs_bucket_name()
    path = os.path.join('/', bucket_name, user.user_id(),
```

```
                        file_name)
    real_path = '/gs' + path
    key = blobstore.create_gs_key(real_path)
    url = images.get_serving_url(key, size=0)
    thumbnail_url = images.get_serving_url(key, size=150,
                                            crop=True)
    return url, thumbnail_url
```

The method takes the filename as a parameter and builds the full path to Cloud Storage with the slightly different /gs/<bucket_name>/<user_id>/<filename> scheme (notice the /gs string that we need to prefix only when generating the encoded key). The real path to the file is then passed to the create_gs_key() function, which generates an encoded key, and then we call the get_serving_url() method twice: once to generate the URL for the full-sized image and then to generate the URL for a cropped thumbnail with a size of 150 pixels. Finally, both the URLs are returned. These URLs will be permanently available unless we call the delete_serving_url() method from the Images service passing the same key. If we don't specify the size parameter, the CDN will serve an optimized version of the image that is smaller in size by default; explicitly passing the size=0 parameter to the first call to the get_serving_url() function will make the CDN serve the original image.

We can improve the data model by providing a new kind that describes a file attached to a note. In the models.py module, we add the following:

```
    class NoteFile(ndb.Model):
        name = ndb.StringProperty()
        url = ndb.StringProperty()
        thumbnail_url = ndb.StringProperty()
        full_path = ndb.StringProperty()
```

We store the name, the two URLs, and the full path in Cloud Storage for each file. We then reference a NoteFile instance instead of the plain filename from the Note model:

```
    class Note(ndb.Model):
        title = ndb.StringProperty()
        content = ndb.TextProperty(required=True)
        date_created = ndb.DateTimeProperty(auto_now_add=True)
        checklist_items = ndb.KeyProperty("CheckListItem",
                                            repeated=True)
        files = ndb.KeyProperty("NoteFile",
                                repeated=True)
```

```
    @classmethod
    def owner_query(cls, parent_key):
        return cls.query(ancestor=parent_key).order(
            -cls.date_created)
```

To store data according to the new model, we refactor the `_create_note()` method:

```
@ndb.transactional
def _create_note(self, user, file_name, file_path):
    note = Note(parent=ndb.Key("User", user.nickname()),
                title=self.request.get('title'),
                content=self.request.get('content'))
    note.put()

    item_titles = self.request.get('checklist_items').split(',')
    for item_title in item_titles:
        item = CheckListItem(parent=note.key, title=item_title)
        item.put()
        note.checklist_items.append(item.key)

    if file_name and file_path:
        url, thumbnail_url = self._get_urls_for(file_name)

        f = NoteFile(parent=note.key, name=file_name,
                     url=url, thumbnail_url=thumbnail_url,
                     full_path=file_path)
        f.put()
        note.files.append(f.key)

    note.put()
```

We generate the URLs and create the `NoteFile` instance, adding it to the `Note` entity group. In the `post()` method of the `MainHandler` class, we now call the `_create_note()` method as follows:

```
self._create_note(user, file_name, real_path)
```

In the HTML template, we add this code:

```
{% if note.files %}
<ul>
  {% for file in note.files %}
  <li class="file">
    <a href="{{ file.get().url }}">
```

```
        <img src="{{ file.get().thumbnail_url }}">
      </a>
    </li>
  {% endfor %}
</ul>
{% endif %}
```

Instead of the name of the file, we show the thumbnail inside a link pointing to the full-sized version of the image.

Serving other types of files

We cannot use the Images service on file types that are not images, so we need to follow a different strategy in this case. Files stored in Cloud Storage that are publicly accessible can be reached by composing the URL of Google CDN with their full path.

The first thing to do, then, is to change the default ACL when we save the files in the `post()` method of the `MainHandler` class:

```
with cloudstorage.open(real_path, 'w', content_type=content_t,
                      options={'x-goog-acl': 'public-read'}) as f:
    f.write(file_content.read())
```

The `options` parameter for the `open()` method of GCS Client Library lets us specify a dictionary of strings containing additional headers to pass to the Cloud Storage service: in this case, we set the `x-goog-acl` header to the `public-read` value so that the file will be publicly available. From now on, we could reach that file with a URL of the `http://storage.googleapis.com/<bucket_name>/<file_path>` type, so let's add the code to compose and store such URLs for files that are not images.

In the `_get_urls_for()` method, we catch errors of the `TransformationError` or `NotImageError` type assuming that if the Images service failed to handle a certain file, that file is not an image:

```
def _get_urls_for(self, file_name):
    user = users.get_current_user()
    if user is None:
        return

    bucket_name = app_identity.get_default_gcs_bucket_name()
    path = os.path.join('/', bucket_name, user.user_id(),
                        file_name)
    real_path = '/gs' + path
    key = blobstore.create_gs_key(real_path)
    try:
```

```
            url = images.get_serving_url(key, size=0)
            thumbnail_url = images.get_serving_url(key, size=150,
                                                  crop=True)
        except images.TransformationError, images.NotImageError:
            url = "http://storage.googleapis.com{}".format(path)
            thumbnail_url = None

        return url, thumbnail_url
```

If the file type is not supported by the Images service, we compose the `url` parameter as stated before and set the `thumbnail_url` variable to the `None` value.

In the HTML template, we will show the filename instead of the thumbnail for files that are not images:

```
{% if note.files %}
<ul>
  {% for file in note.files %}
  {% if file.get().thumbnail_url %}
  <li class="file">
    <a href="{{ file.get().url }}">
      <img src="{{ file.get().thumbnail_url }}">
    </a>
  </li>
  {% else %}
  <li class="file">
    <a href="{{ file.get().url }}">{{ file.get().name }}</a>
  </li>
  {% endif %}
  {% endfor %}
</ul>
{% endif %}
```

Transforming images with the Images service

We already used the App Engine Images service to serve images through Google's CDN, but there's a lot more it can do. It can resize, rotate, flip, crop images, and composite multiple images into a single file. It can enhance pictures using a predefined algorithm. It can convert an image from and to several formats. The service can also provide information about an image, such as its format, width, height, and a histogram of color values.

> To use the Images service on the local development server, we need to download and install the **Python Imaging Library** (**PIL**) package or, alternatively, the `pillow` package.

We can pass the image data to the service directly from our application or specifying a resource stored in Cloud Storage. To see how this works, we add a function to our Notes application that users can trigger to shrink all the images attached to any note in order to save space in Cloud Storage. To do this, we add a dedicated request handler to the `main.py` module, which will be invoked when users hit the `/shrink` URL:

```python
class ShrinkHandler(webapp2.RequestHandler):
    def _shrink_note(self, note):
        for file_key in note.files:
            file = file_key.get()
            try:
                with cloudstorage.open(file.full_path) as f:
                    image = images.Image(f.read())
                    image.resize(640)
                    new_image_data = image.execute_transforms()

                    content_t = images_formats.get(str(image.format))
                    with cloudstorage.open(file.full_path, 'w',
                                          content_type=content_t) as f:
                        f.write(new_image_data)

            except images.NotImageError:
                pass

    def get(self):
        user = users.get_current_user()
        if user is None:
            login_url = users.create_login_url(self.request.uri)
            return self.redirect(login_url)

        ancestor_key = ndb.Key("User", user.nickname())
        notes = Note.owner_query(ancestor_key).fetch()

        for note in notes:
            self._shrink_note(note)

        self.response.write('Done.')
```

Storing and Processing Users' Data

In the `get()` method, we load all the notes belonging to the current logged in user from the Datastore, and then we invoke the `_shrink_note()` method on each of them. For each file attached to a note, we check whether it is an image; if not, we catch the error and pass to the next one. If the file is actually an image, we open the file with GCS Client Library and pass the image data to the `Image` class constructor. Image objects wrap image data and provide an interface to manipulate and get information for the wrapped image. Transformations are not applied immediately; they are added to a queue that is processed when we invoke the `execute_transforms()` method on the `Image` instance. In our case, we apply just one transformation, resizing the image to 640 pixel width. The `execute_transforms()` method returns the transformed image data we use to overwrite the original file. When writing the new image data on Cloud Storage, we need to specify the content type for the file again: we derive the right content type from the `format` property of the `image` object. This value is an integer that has to be mapped to a content type string; we do this by adding this dictionary at the top of the `main.py` module:

```
images_formats = {
    '0': 'image/png',
    '1': 'image/jpeg',
    '2': 'image/webp',
    '-1': 'image/bmp',
    '-2': 'image/gif',
    '-3': 'image/ico',
    '-4': 'image/tiff',
}
```

We cast the `image.format` value to the string and access the right string to pass to the `open()` method from GCS Client Library.

We add the mapping for the `/shrink` URL in the `main.py` module:

```
app = webapp2.WSGIApplication([
    (r'/', MainHandler),
    (r'/media/(?P<file_name>[\w.]{0,256})', MediaHandler),
    (r'/shrink', ShrinkHandler),
], debug=True)
```

To let users access this functionality, we add a hyperlink on the main page. We take the opportunity to provide a main menu for our application, changing the `main.html` template as follows:

```
<h1>Welcome to Notes!</h1>

<ul class="menu">
```

```
    <li>Hello, <b>{{ user }}</b></li>
    <li><a href="{{ logout_url }}">Logout</a></li>
    <li><a href="/shrink">Shrink images</a></li>
</ul>

<form action="" method="post" enctype="multipart/form-data">
```

To make the menu lay out horizontally, we add these lines to the `notes.css` file:

```
ul.menu > li {
    display: inline;
    padding: 5px;
    border-left: 1px solid;
}

ul.menu > li > a {
    text-decoration: none;
}
```

Users can now shrink the space taken by images attached to their notes clicking the corresponding action in the menu on the main page.

Processing long jobs with the task queue

App Engine provides a mechanism called **request timer** to ensure that requests from a client have a finite lifespan, avoiding infinite loops and preventing an overly aggressive use of the resources from an application. In particular, the request timer raises a `DeadlineExceededError` error whenever a request takes more than 60 seconds to complete. We have to take this into consideration if our application provides functionalities that involve complex queries, I/O operations, or image processing. This is the case of the `ShrinkHandler` class from the previous paragraph: the number of notes to be loaded and the attached images to be processed could be big enough to make the request last more than 60 seconds. In such cases, we can use the **task queue**, which is a service provided by App Engine that lets us execute operations outside the request / response cycle with a wider time limit of 10 minutes.

There are two types of task queue: **push queues**, which are used for tasks that are automatically processed by the App Engine infrastructure, and **pull queues**, which let developers build their own task-consuming strategy either with another App Engine application or externally from another infrastructure. We will use push queues so that we have a turnkey solution from App Engine without worrying about the setup and scalability of external components.

We will run the shrink images functionality inside a task queue, and to do so, we need to refactor the `ShrinkHandler` class: in the `get()` method, we will start the task, moving the execution of the query and the image processing to the `post()` method. The `post()` method will be invoked by the task queue consumer infrastructure to process the task.

We first need to import the `taskqueue` package to use the task queue Python API:

```
from google.appengine.api import taskqueue
```

Then, we add the `post()` method to the `ShrinkHandler` class:

```
def post(self):
    if not 'X-AppEngine-TaskName' in self.request.headers:
        self.error(403)

    user_email = self.request.get('user_email')
    user = users.User(user_email)

    ancestor_key = ndb.Key("User", user.nickname())
    notes = Note.owner_query(ancestor_key).fetch()

    for note in notes:
        self._shrink_note(note)
```

To ensure that we have received a task queue request, we check whether the `X-AppEngine-TaskName` HTTP header was set; App Engine strips these kinds of headers if requests come from outside the platform, so we can trust the client. If this header is missing, we set the `HTTP 403: Forbidden` response code.

The request contains a `user_email` parameter containing the e-mail of the user who added this task to the queue (we'll see where this parameter has to be set in a moment); we instance a `User` object by passing the e-mail address to match a valid user and proceed with image processing.

The `get()` method of the `ShrinkHandler` class has to be refactored as follows:

```
def get(self):
    user = users.get_current_user()
    if user is None:
        login_url = users.create_login_url(self.request.uri)
        return self.redirect(login_url)

    taskqueue.add(url='/shrink',
                  params={'user_email': user.email()})
    self.response.write('Task successfully added to the queue.')
```

[64]

After checking whether the user is logged in, we add a task to the queue using the task queue API. We pass the URL mapped to the handler that will perform the job as a parameter and a dictionary containing the parameters we want to pass to the handler. In this case, we set the `user_email` parameter we use in the `post()` method to load a valid `User` instance. After the task is added to the queue, a response is immediately returned, and when executed, the actual shrinking operation could last up to 10 minutes.

Scheduling tasks with Cron

We have designed the shrink operation as an optional functionality triggered by users, but we could run it at a determined time interval for every user in order to lower the costs of Cloud Storage. App Engine supports the scheduled execution of jobs with the Cron service; every application has a limited number of Cron jobs available, depending on our billing plan. Cron jobs have the same restrictions as tasks in a task queue, so the request can last up to 10 minutes.

We first prepare a request handler that will implement the job:

```
class ShrinkCronJob(ShrinkHandler):
    def post(self):
        self.abort(405, headers=[('Allow', 'GET')])

    def get(self):
        if 'X-AppEngine-Cron' not in self.request.headers:
            self.error(403)

        notes = Note.query().fetch()
        for note in notes:
            self._shrink_note(note)
```

We derive the `ShrinkCronJob` class from the `ShrinkHandler` class to inherit the `_shrink_note()` method. The cron service performs an HTTP request of type `GET`, so we should override the `post()` method, simply returning a **HTTP 405: Method not allowed** error, thus avoiding someone hitting our handler with an HTTP `POST` request. All the logic is implemented in the `get()` method of the handler class. To ensure the handler was triggered by the Cron service and not by an external client, we first check whether the request contains the `X-AppEngine-Cron` header that is normally stripped by App Engine; if this is not the case, we return a **HTTP 403: Unauthorized** error. Then, we load all the Note entities from the Datastore and invoke the `_shrink_note()` method on each of them.

We then map the `ShrinkCronJob` handler to the `/shrink_all` URL:

```
app = webapp2.WSGIApplication([
    (r'/', MainHandler),
    (r'/media/(?P<file_name>[\w.]{0,256})', MediaHandler),
    (r'/shrink', ShrinkHandler),
    (r'/shrink_all', ShrinkCronJob),
], debug=True)
```

Cron jobs are listed in a `YAML` file in the application root, so we create the `cron.yaml` file with the following content:

```
cron:
- description: shrink images in the GCS
  url: /shrink_all
  schedule: every day 00:00
```

The file contains a list of job definitions with some properties: for each job, we must specify the URL and `schedule` properties, containing the URL mapped to the handler implementing the job and the time interval at which the job is executed, respectively, every day at midnight. We also add the optional `description` property containing a string to detail the job.

The list of scheduled Cron jobs is updated every time we deploy the application; we can check for jobs' details and status by accessing the Developer Console or the local Development Console.

Sending notification e-mails

It's very common for web applications to send notifications to the users, and e-mails are a cheap and effective channel for delivering. The Notes application could benefit from a notification system as well: early in this chapter, we modified the `shrink` image function so that it runs in a task queue. Users receive a response immediately, but the actual job is put in a queue and they don't know if and when shrink operations complete successfully.

As we can send e-mail messages from an App Engine application on behalf of the administrators or users with Google Accounts, we send a message to the user as soon as the shrink operation is completed.

We first import the mail package in the `main.py` module:

```
from google.appengine.api import mail
```

Then we append the following code to the end of the `post()` method in the `ShrinkHandler` class:

```
sender_address = "Notes Team <notes@example.com>"
subject = "Shrink complete!"
body = "We shrunk all the images attached to your notes!"
mail.send_mail(sender_address, user_email, subject, body)
```

All we have to do is invoke the `send_mail()` method, passing in the sender address, the destination address, the subject of the e-mail, and the body of the message.

If we are running the application on the production server, the `sender_address` parameter must contain the registered address on App Engine of one of the administrators, or the message won't be delivered.

If the application is running on the local development server, App Engine will not send out real e-mails and will show a detailed message on the console instead.

Receiving users' data as e-mail messages

A less common but useful feature for a web application is the ability to receive e-mail messages from its users: for example, a **Customer Relationship Management (CRM)** application could open a support ticket after receiving an e-mail sent out from a user to a certain address, say, `support@example.com`.

To show how this works on App Engine, we add the ability for our users to create notes by sending e-mail messages to the Notes application: the e-mail subject will be used for the title, the message body for the note content, and every file attached to the e-mail message will be stored on Cloud Storage and be attached to the note as well.

App Engine applications can receive e-mail messages at any address of the `<string>@<appid>.appspotmail.com` form; messages are then transformed to HTTP requests to the `/_ah/mail/<address>` URL, where a request handler will process the data.

Before we start, we need to enable the incoming e-mail service, which is disabled by default, so we add the following in our `app.yaml` file:

```
inbound_services:
- mail
```

Storing and Processing Users' Data

Then, we need to implement a handler for the e-mail messages, deriving from a specialized `InboundMailHandler` request handler class provided by App Engine. Our subclass must override the `receive()` method that takes a parameter containing an instance of the `InboundEmailMessage` class that we can use to access all the details from the e-mail message we received. We add this new handler to the `main.py` module but before proceeding, we need to import the modules and packages required:

```
from google.appengine.ext.webapp import mail_handlers
import re
```

Then, we start implementing our `CreateNoteHandler` class; this is the first part of the code:

```
class CreateNoteHandler(mail_handlers.InboundMailHandler):
    def receive(self, mail_message):
        email_pattern = re.compile(
            r'([\w\-\.]+@(\w[\w\-]+\.)+[\w\-]+)')
        match = email_pattern.findall(mail_message.sender)
        email_addr = match[0][0] if match else ''

        try:
            user = users.User(email_addr)
            user = self._reload_user(user)
        except users.UserNotFoundError:
            return self.error(403)

        title = mail_message.subject
        content = ''
        for content_t, body in mail_message.bodies('text/plain'):
            content += body.decode()

        attachments = getattr(mail_message, 'attachments', None)

        self._create_note(user, title, content, attachments)
```

The first part of the code implements a simple security check: we actually create a note for a certain user only if the e-mail message comes from the same address users registered for their account. We first extract the e-mail address from the `sender` field of the `InboundEmailMessage` instance contained in the `mail_message` parameter with a regular expression. We then instance a `User` object representing the owner of the e-mail address that sent the message. If the sender does not correspond to a registered user, App Engine raises a `UserNotFoundError` error and we return a `403: Forbidden` HTTP response code, otherwise we call the `_reload_user()` method.

If users want to attach a file to their notes, the Notes application needs to know the user ID of the note owner to build the path when storing files on Cloud Storage; the problem is that when we programmatically instance a `User` class without calling the `get_current_user()` method from the `users` API, the `user_id()` method of the instance always returns the `None` value. At the time of writing this, App Engine does not provide a clean method to determine the user ID from an instance of the `User` class, so we implement a workaround by following these steps:

1. Assign the `User` instance to a field of a Datastore entity, which is called the `UserLoader` entity.
2. Store the `UserLoader` entity in the Datastore.
3. Immediately after, load the entity again.

This way, we force the `Users` service to fill in all the user data; by accessing the field containing the `User` instance in the `UserLoader` entity, we will get all the user properties, including the `id` property. We perform this operation in a utility method of the handler class:

```
def _reload_user(self, user_instance):
    key = UserLoader(user=user_instance).put()
    key.delete(use_datastore=False)
    u_loader = UserLoader.query(
        UserLoader.user == user_instance).get()
    return UserLoader.user
```

To force a clean reload of the entity from the Datastore, we first need to purge the NDB cache, and we do this by calling the `delete()` method on the key passing the `use_datastore=False` parameter. We then reload the entity from the Datastore and return the `user` property, now containing all the data we need. We add the `UserLoader` model class to our `models.py` module:

```
class UserLoader(ndb.Model):
    user = ndb.UserProperty()
```

Back in the `receive()` method, we proceed to extract all the data we need from the e-mail message after reloading the `User` instance; in order to extract all the data, we need to create a note: the message subject is a simple string that we will use as the note title. Accessing the body is a little bit more complex because e-mail messages might have multiple bodies with different content types, typically plain text or HTML; in this case, we extract only the plain text body and use it as the note content.

In the case, the e-mail messages have attachments, and the `mail_message` instance provides the `attachments` attribute: we pass it as a parameter to the method dedicated to note creation, that is the `_create_note()` method. The `_create_note()` method runs in a transaction and encapsulates all the logic needed to create a `Note` entity:

```
@ndb.transactional
def _create_note(self, user, title, content, attachments):

    note = Note(parent=ndb.Key("User", user.nickname()),
                title=title,
                content=content)
    note.put()

    if attachments:
        bucket_name = app_identity.get_default_gcs_bucket_name()
        for file_name, file_content in attachments:
            content_t = mimetypes.guess_type(file_name)[0]
            real_path = os.path.join('/', bucket_name,
                                    user.user_id(), file_name)

            with cloudstorage.open(real_path, 'w',
                    content_type=content_t,
                    options={'x-goog-acl': 'public-read'}) as f:
                f.write(file_content.decode())

            key = blobstore.create_gs_key('/gs' + real_path)
            try:
                url = images.get_serving_url(key, size=0)
                thumbnail_url = images.get_serving_url(key,
                    size=150, crop=True)
            except images.TransformationError, \
                    images.NotImageError:
                url = "http://storage.googleapis.com{}".format(
                    real_path)
                thumbnail_url = None

            f = NoteFile(parent=note.key, name=file_name,
                        url=url, thumbnail_url=thumbnail_url,
                        full_path=real_path)
            f.put()
            note.files.append(f.key)

        note.put()
```

The method is quite similar to the method that has the same name in the `MainHandler` class; the main difference is the way in which we access data from the files attached to the e-mail message. The `attachments` parameter is a list of tuples of two elements: one is a string containing the file name and the other is an instance of a **wrapper** class containing the message payload. We use the filename to build the full path to the file in Cloud Storage, and we use the `decode()` method to access the payload data and store it in a file.

Finally, we map the URL to the handler:

```
app = webapp2.WSGIApplication([
    (r'/', MainHandler),
    (r'/media/(?P<file_name>[\w.]{0,256})', MediaHandler),
    (r'/shrink', ShrinkHandler),
    (r'/shrink_all', ShrinkCronJob),
    (r'/_ah/mail/<appid>\.appspotmail\.com', CreateNoteHandler),
], debug=True)
```

When testing the application on the local development server, we can use the development console to simulate e-mail sending from a web interface; this function is available from the bar on the left-hand side by clicking on the **Inbound Mail** menu item.

Summary

In this chapter, we pushed a lot of features in our Notes application, and we should now be able to leverage the Cloud Storage and use it to store and serve static contents from our applications. We saw the Images API in action, and we should now know how to deal with requests that take a long time, and we also learned how to schedule recurrent tasks. In the last part, we delved into the Mail API capabilities and we learned how App Engine provides a turnkey solution to send and receive e-mail messages.

In the next chapter, we will take a look at the performance of our application and see where and how we can improve, using advanced features of components we are already using together with more services provided by App Engine.

4
Improving Application Performance

Even if our Notes application lacks many details, at this point, we are using a number of key components of the Cloud Platform, and so it can be considered a fully fledged web application. This is a good opportunity to stop adding major features and trying to delve into some implementation details involving Datastore, Memcache, and the Modules service in order to optimize application performance.

While going through this chapter, we have to take into consideration how optimizing a web application running on a pay-per-use service such as App Engine is crucial both to maximize performance and lower costs.

In this chapter, we will cover the following topics:

- Gain a deeper knowledge of Datastore: properties, queries, caching, indexing and administration
- How to store transient data into Memcache
- How to structure our application with the help of the Modules service

Advanced use of Datastore

We have already learned a lot about Datastore so far, including how to define entity kinds with model classes, the property concept, and how to make simple queries.

There is a lot more we can do with the NDB Python API to optimize an application, as we will see shortly.

More on properties – arrange composite data with StructuredProperty

In our Notes application, we defined the `CheckListItem` model class to represent checkable items, and then we added a property to the `Note` model named `checklist_items` that references a list of that kind of entities. This is what we usually call a one-to-many relationship between notes and checklist items, and it is a common way to structure application data. By following this strategy, though, every time we add an item to a note, we have to create and store a new entity on Datastore. This is not a bad practice at all, but we have to take into consideration that we are charged for the use of Datastore depending on the number of operations we make; so, if we have a lot of data, keeping a low rate of write operations can potentially save a lot of money.

The Python NDB API provides a property type called `StructuredProperty` we can use to include one kind of model inside another; instead of referencing the `CheckListItem` model from a property of the type `KeyProperty` in the `Note` model, we store it in a property of the type `StructuredProperty`. In our `models.py` module, we change the Note model as follows:

```
class Note(ndb.Model):
    title = ndb.StringProperty()
    content = ndb.TextProperty(required=True)
    date_created = ndb.DateTimeProperty(auto_now_add=True)
    checklist_items = ndb.StructuredProperty(CheckListItem,
                                             repeated=True)
    files = ndb.KeyProperty("NoteFile", repeated=True)
```

In the `main.py` module, we need to adjust the code to store checklist items when we create a new note, so we refactor the `create_note` method in this way:

```
@ndb.transactional
def _create_note(self, user, file_name, file_path):
    note = Note(parent=ndb.Key("User", user.nickname()),
                title=self.request.get('title'),
                content=self.request.get('content'))

    item_titles = self.request.get('checklist_items').split(',')
    for item_title in item_titles:
        if not item_title:
            continue
        item = CheckListItem(title=item_title)
```

```
        note.checklist_items.append(item)
    note.put()

    if file_name and file_path:
        url, thumbnail_url = self._get_urls_for(file_name)

        f = NoteFile(parent=note.key, name=file_name,
                     url=url, thumbnail_url=thumbnail_url,
                     full_path=file_path)
        f.put()
        note.files.append(f.key)
        note.put()
```

First of all, we move the call to the `note.put()` method right below the note creation; we don't need to provide a valid key to the `parent` parameter in the `CheckListItem` constructor, so we can persist the `Note` instance later, at the end of the method. We then instance a `CheckListItem` object for every item we want to add to the note as before, but without actually creating any entity in Datastore; these objects will be transparently serialized by the NDB API within the `Note` entity.

We need to adjust the HTML template as well, as the `checklist_items` property in notes entities does not contain a list of keys anymore; it contains a list of `CheckListItem` objects instead. In the `main.html` file, we change the code accordingly, removing the `get()` method calls:

```
{% if note.checklist_items %}
<ul>
  {% for item in note.checklist_items %}
  <li class="{%if item.checked%}checked{%endif%}">
    {{item.title}}
  </li>
  {% endfor %}
</ul>
{% endif %}
```

To see how it's easy to work with structured properties, we add a very small feature to the app: a link to toggle the checked status for items in checklists. To toggle the status of an item, we have to provide the request handler with the key of the note containing the item and the index of the item itself inside the `checklist_items` list, so we build a URL with the scheme `/toggle/<note_key>/<item_index>`. In the `main.html` file, we add this:

```
{% if note.checklist_items %}
<ul>
  {% for item in note.checklist_items %}
```

```
        <li class="{%if item.checked%}checked{%endif%}">
          <a href="/toggle/{{note.key.urlsafe()}}/{{ loop.index }}">
            {{item.title}}
          </a>
        </li>
      {% endfor %}
    </ul>
  {% endif %}
```

Instances of the `Key` class have a `urlsafe()` method that serializes key objects into a string that can be safely used as part of URLs. To retrieve the current index inside a loop, we use the `loop.index` expression provided by Jinja2. We can also add a simple CSS rule to the `notes.css` file to make the items look a little better:

```
div.note > ul > li > a {
    text-decoration: none;
    color: inherit;
}
```

To implement the toggling logic, we add the `ToggleHandler` class in the `main.py` module:

```
class ToggleHandler(webapp2.RequestHandler):
    def get(self, note_key, item_index):
        item_index = int(item_index) - 1
        note = ndb.Key(urlsafe=note_key).get()
        item = note.checklist_items[item_index]
        item.checked = not item.checked
        note.put()
        self.redirect('/')
```

We normalize the item index so that it is zero-based, and then we load a note entity from Datastore using its key. We instantiate a `Key` object passing the string generated with the `urlsafe()` method to the constructor with the `urlsafe` keyword parameter, then we retrieve the entity with the `get()` method. After toggling the state of the item at the requested index, we update the note content in Datastore calling the `put()` method. We finally redirect users to the main page of the application.

Eventually, we add the URL mapping to the application constructor with a regular expression matching our URL scheme, `/toggle/<note_key>/<item_index>`:

```
app = webapp2.WSGIApplication([
    (r'/', MainHandler),
    (r'/media/(?P<file_name>[\w.]{0,256})', MediaHandler),
    (r'/shrink', ShrinkHandler),
    (r'/shrink_all', ShrinkCronJob),
```

```
    (r'/toggle/(?P<note_key>[\w\-]+)/(?P<item_index>\d+)',
ToggleHandler),
    (r'/_ah/mail/create@book-123456\.appspotmail\.com',
CreateNoteHandler),
], debug=True)
```

Working with structured properties is straightforward; we simply access properties and fields of the objects contained in the `checklist_items` property as they were actual entities.

The only drawback of this approach is that `CheckListItem` entities are not actually stored in Datastore; they don't have a key and we cannot load them independently from the `Note` entity they belong to, but this is perfectly fine for our use case. Instead of loading the `CheckListItem` entity we want to update, we load the `Note` entity and we use the index to access the item. In exchange, during notes creation, we save a `put()` method call for the note and a `put()` method call for each item in the checklist and when retrieving a note, we save a `get()` method call for each item in the checklist. Needless to say, this kind of optimization can impact favorably on application costs.

More on queries – save space with projections and optimize iterations with mapping

Queries are used within an application to search Datastore for entities that match a search criteria we can define through filters. We have already used Datastore queries to retrieve entities with a filter; for example, every time we perform an ancestor query, we are actually filtering out these entities that have a different parent from the one we provided to the NDB API `query()` function.

There is much more we can do with query filters though, and in this section, we will see, in detail, two features provided by the NDB API that can be used to optimize application performance: projection queries and mapping.

Projection queries

When we retrieve an entity with a query, we get all the properties and data for that entity as expected; sometimes though, after retrieving an entity, we use a small subset of its data. For example, take the `post()` method in our `ShrinkHandler` class; we perform an ancestor query to retrieve only the notes belonging to the currently logged in user, then we invoke the `_shrink_note()` method on each of them. The `_shrink_note()` method only accesses the `files` property from note entities, so we are keeping in memory and passing around a rather large object even if we only need a very small part of it.

With the NDB API, we can pass a projection parameter to the `fetch()` method that contains a list of properties we want to be set for the entities retrieved. For example, in the `post()` method of the `ShrinkHandler` class, we can modify the code in this way:

```
notes = Note.owner_query(ancestor_key).fetch(
    projection=[Note.files])
```

This is a so-called projection query and the entities fetched in this way will have only the `files` property set. The fetch is much more efficient because it retrieves and serializes less data and entities use less space while in memory. If we try to access any other property than `files` on such entities, an `UnprojectedPropertyError` error will be raised.

Projections have some limitations we must be aware of. First of all, as we can expect, entities fetched with a projection cannot be saved back on Datastore because they are only partially populated. Another limitation is regarding indexes; in fact, we can only specify indexed properties in a projection and this makes it impossible to project properties with unindexed types such as the `TextProperty` type.

Mapping

Sometimes, we need to call the same function on a set of entities returned by a query. For example, in the `post()` method of the `ShrinkHandler` class, we need to call the `_shrink_note()` method on all the note entities for the current user:

```
ancestor_key = ndb.Key("User", user.nickname())
notes = Note.owner_query(ancestor_key).fetch()
for note in notes:
    self._shrink_note(note)
```

We first fetch all the entities matching the query in the notes list, then we call the same function for every item in the list. We can rewrite that code replacing the `for` iteration with a single call to the `map()` method provided by the NDB API:

```
ancestor_key = ndb.Key("User", user.nickname())
Note.owner_query(ancestor_key).map(self._shrink_note)
```

We call the `map()` method passing the callback function we want to be called on each result of the query; the callback function receives an entity object of kind Note as its only parameter, unless we invoke the `map()` method with the `keys_only=True` parameter. In this case, the callback will receive a `Key` instance when invoked.

Since the `map()` method accepts the standard set of query options (that's why we can pass the `keys_only` parameter), we can perform the mapping for a projection query too:

```
Note.owner_query(ancestor_key).map(
    self._shrink_note, projection=[Note.files])
```

Besides the projection, this version of the code is slightly more efficient because the Datastore can apply some concurrency while loading entities and the results are retrieved in batches instead of fetching the entire dataset in memory. If we want to get information regarding the current batch inside the callback function, we need to pass the `pass_batch_into_callback=True` parameter when calling the `map()` method. In this case, the callback will receive three parameters: a `Batch` object provided by App Engine that wraps a lot of information about the current batch, the index of the current item inside the current batch, and the entity object (or the entity key if the `keys_only` parameter was used) fetched from Datastore.

NDB asynchronous operations

As we can expect, Datastore is a key component when considering application performance; adjusting queries and using the right idioms can dramatically improve efficiency and lower costs but there's more. Thanks to the NDB API, we can speed up our applications by performing Datastore actions in parallel with other jobs, or performing a number of Datastore actions concurrently.

Several functions provided by the NDB API have an `_async` counterpart that takes exactly the same arguments, such as the `put` and `put_async` functions. Every async function returns a **future**, an object that represents an operation that was started but possibly not completed. We get the result of an async operation from the future itself calling the `get_result()` method.

In our Notes application, we can use asynchronous operations in the `_render_template()` method of the `MainHandler` class:

```
def _render_template(self, template_name, context=None):
    if context is None:
        context = {}

    user = users.get_current_user()
    ancestor_key = ndb.Key("User", user.nickname())
    qry = Note.owner_query(ancestor_key)
    context['notes'] = qry.fetch()

    template = jinja_env.get_template(template_name)
    return template.render(context)
```

Improving Application Performance

Currently, we wait for the notes to be fetched before loading the template but we can load the template while Datastore is working:

```
def _render_template(self, template_name, context=None):
    if context is None:
        context = {}

    user = users.get_current_user()
    ancestor_key = ndb.Key("User", user.nickname())
    qry = Note.owner_query(ancestor_key)
    future = qry.fetch_async()

    template = jinja_env.get_template(template_name)

    context['notes'] = future.get_result()
    return template.render(context)
```

In this way, the application doesn't block on fetching data because the `fetch_async()` method returns immediately; we then proceed loading the template while the Datastore is working. When it's time to fill the context variable, we call the `get_result()` method on the future object. At this point, either the result is available and we proceed with rendering operations, or the `get_result()` method blocks, waiting for Datastore to be ready. In both cases, we managed to perform two tasks in parallel, thereby increasing the performance.

With the NDB API, we can also implement asynchronous tasks called **tasklets** that return a future while performing other work. For example, earlier in this chapter, we used the `map()` method in the `ShrinkHandler` class to call the same function on a set of entities retrieved from Datastore. We know that code is slightly more efficient than the version with the explicit `for` iteration, but it's not much faster actually; the callback function blocks on a synchronous `get()` method, so every step of the mapping waits for the previous to finish.

If we turn the callback function into a tasklet, App Engine can run the mapping in parallel, dramatically speeding up application performance. Writing tasklets is simple, thanks to the NDB API; for example the `_shrink_note()` method of the `ShrinkHandler` class can be transformed in a tasklet with just two lines of code, as follows:

```
@ndb.tasklet
def _shrink_note(self, note):
    for file_key in note.files:
        file = yield file_key.get_async()
        try:
```

```
            with cloudstorage.open(file.full_path) as f:
                image = images.Image(f.read())
                image.resize(640)
                new_image_data = image.execute_transforms()

            content_t = images_formats.get(str(image.format))
            with cloudstorage.open(file.full_path, 'w',
                                  content_type=content_t) as f:
                f.write(new_image_data)

        except images.NotImageError:
            pass
```

We first apply the `ndb.tasklet` decorator to the function we want to turn into a tasklet; the decorator provides all the logic to support the future mechanism with the `get_result()` method. We then use the `yield` statement to tell App Engine that we will suspend at that point of the execution, waiting for the result of the `get_async()` method. While we suspend, the `map()` method can execute another tasklet with a different entity instead of waiting for us to finish.

Caching

Caching is a critical component on a system such as App Engine because it impacts on application performance and Datastore roundtrips and thus on application costs. The NDB API automatically manages the cache for us and provides a set of tools to configure the caching system. It's important to understand how NDB cache works if we want to take advantage of such features.

NDB uses two caching levels: the **in-context** cache that runs in process memory and a gateway to the App Engine Memcache service. The in-context cache stores data only for the duration of a single HTTP request and is local to the code that processes the request, so it is extremely fast. When we use a NDB function to write data on the Datastore, it first populates the in-context cache. Symmetrically, when we use a NDB function to fetch an entity from Datastore, it first searches for it in the in-context cache without even accessing Datastore in the best-case scenario.

Memcache is slower than the in-context cache but still way faster than Datastore. By default, every Datastore operation performed outside a transaction is cached on Memcache and App Engine ensures that data resides on the same server to maximize performance. The NDB ignores Memcache when it operates inside a transaction but when a transaction is committed, it will attempt to remove all the entities involved from Memcache, and we must take into account that some of these deletions can fail.

Both the caches are managed by a so-called context, represented by an instance of the class `Context` provided by App Engine. Each incoming HTTP request and each transaction is executed in a new context, and we can access the current context using the `get_context()` method provided by the NDB API.

In our Notes application, we've already experienced one of these rare situations where NDB automatic caching is actually an issue; in the `_reload_user()` method in `CreateNoteHandler` class, we had to force a reload of the `UserLoader` entity from Datastore as a workaround to populate a `User` object. Between the `put()` method and the `get()` method of the `UserLoader` entity, we wrote this instruction to remove the entity from any location except Datastore:

```
UserLoader(user=user_instance).put()
key.delete(use_datastore=False)
u_loader = UserLoader.query(
    UserLoader.user == user_instance).get()
```

Without this instruction, the NDB caching system would not have fetched the entity from Datastore from scratch as we needed. Now that we know how NDB caching works, we can rewrite that method in an equivalent way, thus being more explicit about cache management, using the `Context` instance:

```
ctx = ndb.get_context()
ctx.set_cache_policy(lambda key: key.kind() != 'UserLoader')
UserLoader(user=user_instance).put()
u_loader = UserLoader.query(
    UserLoader.user == user_instance).get()
```

The `set_cache_policy()` method exposed by the context object accepts a key object and returns a Boolean result. When the method returns the `False` parameter, the entity identified by that key won't be saved in any cache; in our case, we return the `False` parameter only when the entity is of the kind `UserLoader`.

Backup and restore functionalities

In order to use the backup and restore functionalities provided by App Engine for Datastore, we first need to enable **Datastore Admin**, which is disabled by default. Datastore Admin is a web application that provides a set of tools very useful for administrative tasks. At the time writing this, the only way to enable and access Datastore Admin is via the old Admin Console available at https://appengine.google.com.

We access the console for our project and then we have to perform the
following steps:

1. Click on the **Datastore Admin** menu under the **Data** section on the left
   of the page.
2. Click on the button to enable the admin.
3. Select one or more entity kinds we want to backup or restore.

To perform a complete backup, we first have to put our application in read-only
mode. From the console, we need to perform the following steps:

1. Click on **Application Settings** under the **Administration** menu on the left.
2. At the bottom of the page, click on the **Disable Writes...** button under the
   Disable Datastore Writes option.
3. Return to the **Datastore Admin** section and select all the entity kinds we
   want to backup.
4. Click on the **Backup Entities** button.
5. Select the destination of the backup and choose between **blobstore** and
   Cloud Storage. Specify a name for the backup file.
6. Click on the **Backup Entities** button.
7. The backup runs in the background; once finished, it is listed in
   Datastore Admin.
8. Re-enable writings for our application.

From Datastore Admin, we can select a backup and perform a restore. After starting
a restore operation, Datastore Admin will ask us which entity kinds we want to
restore, and then it'll proceed in background.

Indexing

Indexes are tables that list Datastore entities in a sequence determined by certain
properties of the index and optionally by entities' ancestors. Every time we write
on Datastore, indexes are updated to reflect the changes to their respective entities;
when we read from Datastore, results are fetched accessing indexes. This is basically
the reason why reading from Datastore is way much faster than writing.

Our Notes application performs several queries, which means that some index must
be in place, but we have never directly managed or created indexes. This is because
of two reasons. The first reason is that when we run the local development server,
it scans our source code, searching for queries and automatically generates the code
to create all the indexes needed. The other reason is that Datastore automatically
generates basic indexes called predefined indexes for each property of every kind,
functional for simple queries.

Improving Application Performance

Indexes are declared in the `index.yaml` file at the application root with the following syntax:

```
- kind: Note
  ancestor: yes
  properties:
  - name: date_created
    direction: desc
  - name: NoteFile
```

These are the properties needed to define and create the index that allows us to perform queries against Note entities that belong to the currently logged-in user and sort them in reverse by date. When we deploy the application, the `index.yaml` file is uploaded and App Engine starts to build the indexes.

If our application exercises every possible kind of query, including every sorting combination, then the entries generated by the development server will represent a complete set of indexes. This is why, in the vast majority of the cases, we don't need to declare indexes or customize existing ones unless we have a very special case to deal with. Anyway, in order to optimize our application, we can disable indexing for properties we know we will never make a query on. Predefined indexes are not listed in the `index.yaml` file but we can use the properties' constructors inside the `models.py` module to disable them. For example, if we know in advance that we will never search for `NoteFile` entities directly with a query, we can disable indexing for all its properties:

```
class NoteFile(ndb.Model):
    name = ndb.StringProperty(indexed=False)
    url = ndb.StringProperty(indexed=False)
    thumbnail_url = ndb.StringProperty(indexed=False)
    full_path = ndb.StringProperty(indexed=False)
```

By passing the `indexed=False` parameter to constructors, we avoid App Engine to create indexes for those properties so that every time we store a `NoteFile` entity, there will be less indexes to update, speeding up writing operations. The `NoteFile` entities can be still retrieved from the `files` property within the `Note` entity because App Engine will keep on creating the predefined index to retrieve entities by kind and key.

Using Memcache

We already know that Memcache is the distributed in-memory data cache provided by App Engine. A typical use case would be to use it as a cache for rapid data retrieval from persistent storage such as Datastore, but we already know that the NDB API does this for us, so there's no need to explicitly cache entities.

Data stored in Memcache can be evicted at any time, so we should cache only data that we can safely lose without affecting integrity. For example, in our Notes application, we can cache the total number of notes globally stored for every user and display this nice kind of metric on the home page. We can perform a Datastore query counting Note entities every time a user visits the main page but this would be cumbersome, possibly nullifying every optimization we made so far. A better strategy would be to keep a counter in the Memcache and increment that counter every time a note is created within the application; if Memcache data expires, we make the counting query again without losing any data and start over incrementing the in-memory counter.

We implement two functions to wrap Memcache operations: one to get the value of the counter and another to increment it. We first create a new Python module in the utils.py file that contains the following code:

```
from google.appengine.api import memcache
from models import Note
def get_note_counter():
    data = memcache.get('note_count')
    if data is None:
        data = Note.query().count()
        memcache.set('note_count', data)

    return data
```

We first try to access counter value from Memcache calling the get() method asking for the note_count key. If the return value is None, we assume the key is not in cache and we proceed querying Datastore. We then store the result of the query in Memcache and return that value.

We want to display the counter on the main page, so we add it to the template context in the `_render_template()` method of the `MainHandler` class:

```
def _render_template(self, template_name, context=None):
    if context is None:
        context = {}
    user = users.get_current_user()
    ancestor_key = ndb.Key("User", user.nickname())
    qry = Note.owner_query(ancestor_key)
    future = qry.fetch_async()

    template = jinja_env.get_template(template_name)

    context['notes'] = future.get_result()
    context['note_count'] = get_note_counter()

    return template.render(context)
```

Before using the function to get the counter, we need to import it from the `main` module:

```
from utils import get_note_counter
```

We have to modify the HTML template as well:

```
<body>
  <div class="container">

    <h1>Welcome to Notes!</h1>
    <h5>{{ note_count }} notes stored so far!</h5>
```

We can then refresh the main page of the Notes application to see the counter in action. Now it's time to write the code that increments the counter, but there's something we should be aware of before proceeding.

Multiple requests can try to increment the value in Memcache concurrently, potentially causing race conditions. To avoid this scenario, Memcache provides two functions, `incr()` and `decr()`, which atomically increment and decrement a 64-bit integer value. These would be perfectly suitable for our counter but we can provide a more general solution that works also for cache values that are not integers using the **compare** and **set** feature of the App Engine Python API.

In the `utils.py` module, we add the following function:

```
def inc_note_counter():
    client = memcache.Client()
    retry = 0
    while retry < 10:
        data = client.gets('note_count')
        if client.cas('note_count', data+1):
            break
        retry += 1
```

We use an instance of the `Client` class because the compare and set functionalities are not provided as functions in the `memcache` module. After getting a `Client` instance, we enter the so-called `retry` loop that we reiterate up to 10 times if we detect a rare condition. We then try to get the value for the `note_count` key using the `gets` method of the client. This method alters the internal state of the client storing a timestamp value provided by the Memcache service. We then try to increment the value corresponding to the same key calling the `cas()` method on the client object; the method transmits the new value for the key to Memcache, plus the previously mentioned timestamp. If the timestamp matches, the value is updated and the `cas()` method returns the `True` parameter causing the `retry` loop to exit; otherwise, it returns the `False` parameter and we try again.

After importing the `inc_note_counter()` function in the main module, we can call it to increment the counter wherever we create a new note: within the `_create_note` of the `MainHandler` class and within the `_create_note` method in the `CreateNoteHandler` class.

Breaking our application into modules

At the moment, our Notes application provides some frontend functionalities such as serving the main page, together with backend functionalities such as handling cron jobs. This is fine for most use cases but if the application architecture is complex and we have a lot of traffic, having several backend jobs around that steal resources from the frontend cannot be always acceptable. To face this kind of problems, App Engine provides an extremely flexible way to lay out a web application with the use of **modules**.

Every App Engine application is made up of at least on module; even if we didn't already know it, so far we have worked on the default module of our Notes application. A module is identified by a name, consists of source code and configuration files, and can reside in the application root or in a subfolder. Every module has a version and we can deploy multiple versions of the same module; each version will spawn one or more App Engine instances depending on how we configured it for scaling. The ability to deploy multiple versions of the same module, in particular, is very useful for testing new components or deploying progressive upgrades. Modules that are part of the same application share services such as Memcache, Datastore, and task queues, and can communicate in a secure fashion using the modules of the Python API.

To delve into some other detail, we can refactor our Notes application by adding a new module solely dedicated to handle cron jobs. We don't need to add any feature; we just break up and refactor existing code. As the architecture of our application is very simple, we can add the module directly in the application root. First of all, we need to configure this new module, we will name backend inside a new file, backend.yaml, which contains the following:

```
application: notes
module: backend
version: 1
runtime: python27
api_version: 1
threadsafe: yes

handlers:
- url: .*
  script: backend.app
```

This is quite similar to any application configuration file, but the main difference is the module property that contains the name of the module. When this property is not in the configuration file, or it contains the default string as value, App Engine assumes this is the default module for the application. We then tell App Engine we want the app application from the backend_main file Python module handle every request the module will receive. When we do not specify any scaling option in the configuration file, **automatic scaling** will be assumed.

We write a brand new Python module with a dedicated WSGI-compliant application in the backend_main.py file:

```
app = webapp2.WSGIApplication([
    (r'/shrink_all', ShrinkCronJob),
], debug=True)
```

As we see from the mapping, this application will only handle requests for the shrink cron job. We take the handler code from the main module, and to avoid depending on it, we rewrite the `ShrinkCronJob` class so that it doesn't need to derive from the `ShrinkHandler` class anymore. Again, in the `backend_main.py` module, we add the following:

```
class ShrinkCronJob(webapp2.RequestHandler):
    @ndb.tasklet
    def _shrink_note(self, note):
        for file_key in note.files:
            file = yield file_key.get_async()
            try:
                with cloudstorage.open(file.full_path) as f:
                    image = images.Image(f.read())
                    image.resize(640)
                    new_image_data = image.execute_transforms()

                content_t = images_formats.get(str(image.format))
                with cloudstorage.open(file.full_path, 'w',
                                      content_type=content_t) as f:
                    f.write(new_image_data)

            except images.NotImageError:
                pass

    def get(self):
        if 'X-AppEngine-Cron' not in self.request.headers:
            self.error(403)

        notes = Note.query().fetch()
        for note in notes:
            self._shrink_note(note)
```

For convenience, we can move the `image_formats` dictionary into the `utils.py` module so that we can reuse it from here and from the `main.py` module.

Now that we have two modules, we need to route the requests coming to our application to the right module, and we can do this by creating a file called `dispatch.yaml` in the application root that contains the following:

```
dispatch:

  - url: "*/shrink_all"
    module: backend

  - url: "*/*"
    module: default
```

Basically, this is the highest level URL mapping we can have on App Engine. We can use wildcards instead of a regular expression to route URLs of incoming requests to the right module; in this case, we route requests to the `/shrink_all` URL to the backend module, leaving all the rest to the default module.

> Ideally, we could have moved to the backend module also the code implementing notes creation by e-mail but unfortunately App Engine only allows inbound services on default modules.

Working with modules, both on the local development environment and on production, adds some complications because we cannot use the App Engine Launcher graphical interface to start and stop the development server or deploy the application; we must use the command-line tools instead.

For example, we can check out how modules works in the local environment, but we have to start the development server passing the YAML files for each module together with the `dispatch.yaml` file as arguments. In our case, we issue the following on the command line:

`dev_appserver.py app.yaml backend.yaml dispatch.yaml`

To deploy the application on App Engine, we use the `appcfg` command-line tool passing the YAML files of the modules we want to deploy, making sure that the configuration file of the default module is the first of the list during the very first deploy, for example we can use the YAML files as follows:

`appcfg.py update app.yaml backend.yaml`

When the application restarts, we should be able to see an instance running for the additional backend module using Development Console or Admin Console.

> Since working with modules on a small application such as Notes is less practical and provides no benefits for the purpose of the book, we can switch back to the layout with only one module.

Summary

In this chapter, we delved into several details of most of the Cloud Platform components we have used so far. As mentioned before, when using a pay-per-use service such as the Cloud Platform, mastering the details and the best practices provides benefits for performance as well as costs. The majority of this chapter was dedicated to Cloud Datastore, confirming that this is a critical component for almost any web application; knowing how to lay out data or perform queries can determine the success of our application.

We also learned how to safely use Memcache from a Python application, avoiding race conditions and strange behaviors that are difficult to debug. In the last part of the chapter, we covered the modules features of App Engine; even if we have to work on a complex application to completely appreciate the benefits of a modular architecture, knowing what modules are and what they can do for us is an important piece of information if we want to deploy our applications on App Engine.

The next chapter is completely dedicated to the Google Cloud SQL service. We will learn how to create and manage database instances and how to make connections and perform queries.

5
Storing Data in Google Cloud SQL

Google Cloud SQL is a MySQL database server instance that lives in the Google cloud infrastructure; it can be used from outside Google Cloud Platform within applications that don't run on the App Engine platform. We will learn how to use it both ways: by adding code to our Notes application and creating a standalone script that runs on our workstation.

Google offers two billing plans for Cloud SQL, **Packages** and **Per Use**, without providing any free tier. This means we have to pay to execute the code in this chapter, though choosing the Per Use plan and running the instance for the sole purpose of going through the chapter should be extremely cheap.

In this chapter, we will cover the following topics:

- How to create, configure, and run a Cloud SQL instance
- How to manage a running instance
- How to use Cloud SQL from App Engine
- How to use Cloud SQL from outside App Engine

Creating a Cloud SQL instance

We will make heavy use of Developer Console throughout this chapter, and we start by creating an instance of a Cloud SQL database. As we already know from *Chapter 1*, *Getting Started*, even if we created our Notes application from App Engine Admin Console, we should have a corresponding project on Developer Console.

Storing Data in Google Cloud SQL

> At this point, we must have enabled the billing feature for our project to access all the Cloud-SQL-related functionalities from within Developer Console.

From Developer Console, once our project is selected, we have to perform the following:

1. Click the **Cloud SQL** item under the **Storage** section on the left-hand side menu.
2. Push the **Create an instance** button.
3. Provide a name for the database instance, for example, **myfirst**; the name of the instance must be unique within a project and will be always combined with the project name.
4. Select **REGION**, the same as the location of the App Engine application (most likely **United States**).
5. Select a tier for the instance; we can safely use the cheapest tier for the purpose of this chapter, the one labeled **D0**.
6. Click on the **Save** button.

The following screenshot shows Developer Console:

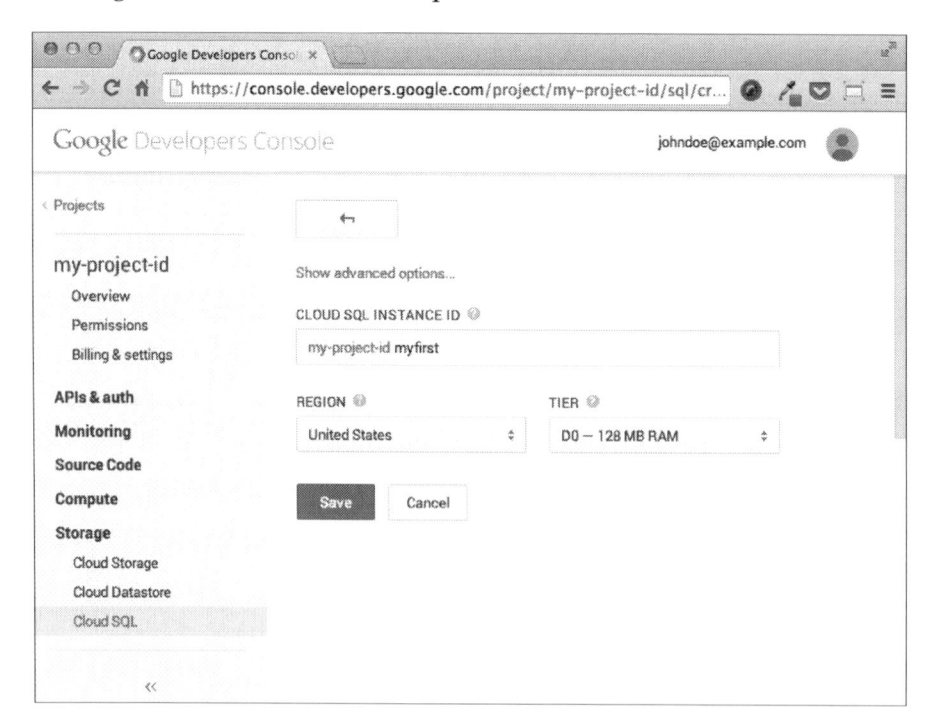

The creation process for our Cloud SQL instance will immediately start. In a few minutes, the status of the instance will become runnable, which means that we can start the instance whenever we need it. We're not charged of any fee while the instance is in the runnable state.

Configuring access

Before using our database instance, we should configure access permissions and credentials to control who can perform connections to the database and how. There are two levels of access control, one at the Cloud Platform level and another at the database level. The first level authorizes access to the Cloud SQL instance from client applications, either from the App Engine infrastructure by checking the application ID, or from a remote node on the Internet by checking the source IP address. The second level is the MySQL privilege system that is responsible for authentication of users and associate them with privileges on databases, such as the ability to perform the SELECT, INSERT, UPDATE or DELETE operation.

If we created the Cloud SQL instance from within our project settings in Developer Console, our App Engine application is already authorized to connect to the database. To double-check, on Developer Console we have to:

1. Click on **Cloud SQL** menu item.
2. Click on the instance ID.
3. Open the **Access Control** tab.

Under the **Authorized App Engine Applications** label, we can see whether our application ID is listed.

While we are on that page, we can set up the access for our local machine; this is needed to perform administrative tasks such as adding users and databases using any MySQL client. We first need to assign an IP address for our instance so that we can reach it from outside the Cloud Platform infrastructure; click the **Add new** link, next to the **IP Addresses** label and wait for the address to be assigned to our instance.

> When we request an IP address for Cloud SQL instances, we should be aware that we will be charged for the time we use this address while instances are not running. To lower costs, we can release the IP address as soon as we don't need it.

Storing Data in Google Cloud SQL

When we connect from our local machine to the Cloud SQL instance, we are obviously outside the App Engine infrastructure, so we have to add our public IP address to the list of the hosts allowed to access from the Internet. For this, we need to perform the following:

1. Get our public IP address; we can use Google for this by hitting this `https://www.google.com/#q=my-ip` URL.
2. Click on the **Add new** link next to the **Authorized Networks** label.
3. Fill out the form with our public IP address.
4. Click on the **Add** button.

The following screenshot shows Developer Console:

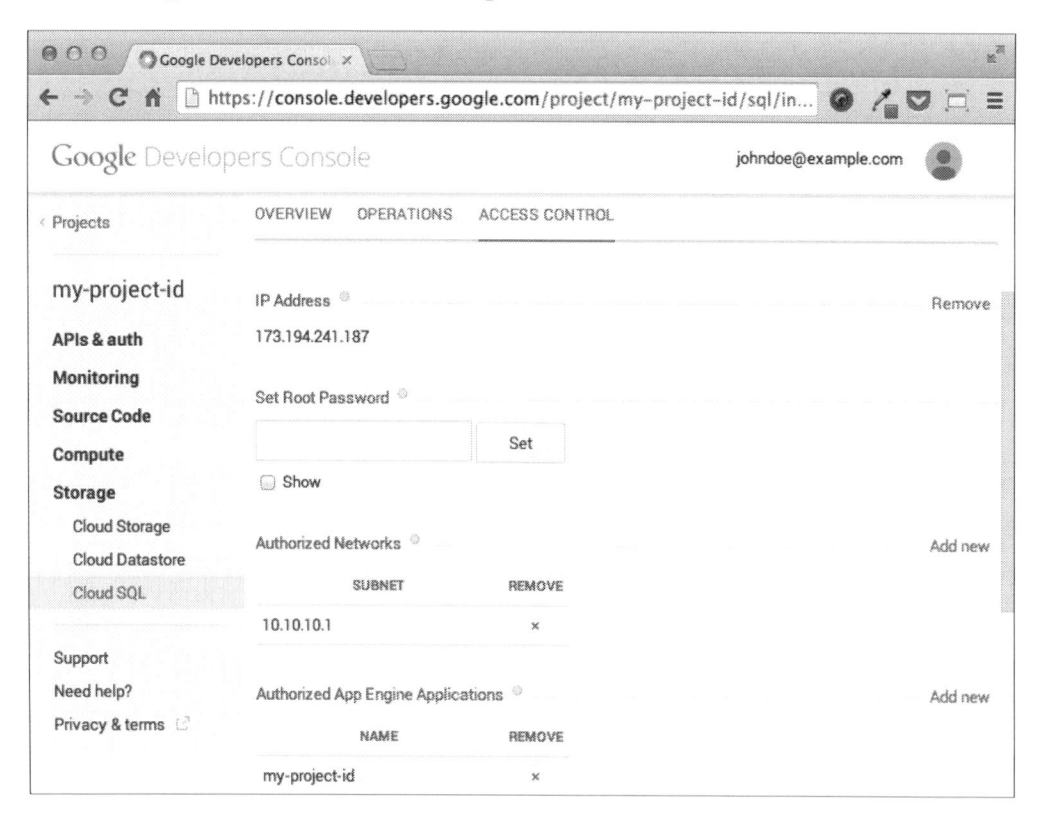

From now on, we can connect to our Cloud SQL instance using the MySQL command line client, for instance, from our laptop. For the first level of the access control system, that's enough for now; we can proceed to configuring the second level.

Setting the root password

The first step to take full control of our Cloud SQL instance is setting a password for the MySQL `root` user; to do this, perform the following:

1. On Developer Console, we go to the **ACCESS CONTROL** tab page.
2. Fill the field under the **Set Root Password** section with the desired password.
3. Click on the **Set** button.

In the next paragraph, we will see how to connect to the instance as a `root` user and perform the administrative tasks we need to complete before using the instance from within our Notes application.

Connecting to the instance with the MySQL console

To interact with our Cloud SQL instance, we will use the MySQL command line client, which is available for all the platforms supported by App Engine, even if we can use any client we feel more comfortable with. The client is usually shipped together with most MySQL server installation packages; besides having the MySQL client tool installed, it is advisable to install MySQL and have a local server running so that we can work with it instead of the production instance while developing applications. We will get back to this soon in this chapter.

Creating the notes database

The first task we need to perform is creating a new database on the Cloud SQL instance; we will use this to store data from our Notes application. To connect to the instance, we issue the following from the command line:

```
mysql -host=<your instance IP> --user=root -password
```

After inserting the password for the `root` user, we should get into the MySQL monitor and see an output similar to the following:

```
Welcome to the MySQL monitor.  Commands end with ; or \g.
Your MySQL connection id is 1
Server version: 5.5.38 (Google)


Copyright (c) 2000, 2014, Oracle and/or its affiliates. All rights
reserved.
```

```
Oracle is a registered trademark of Oracle Corporation and/or its
affiliates. Other names may be trademarks of their respective
owners.

Type 'help;' or '\h' for help. Type '\c' to clear the current input
statement.

mysql>
```

If we successfully managed to get to the prompt, we can create a database named notes by issuing the following instructions:

```
mysql> CREATE DATABASE notes;
Query OK, 1 row affected (1.62 sec)
```

The output of the command should be very similar to the previous command in the case of success; we can now proceed to creating a dedicated database user we will use to perform connections from our Notes application.

Creating a dedicated user

The root user in a MySQL installation has unlimited privileges and it is a good security practice to avoid connecting to the server with the superuser credentials. For this reason, we create a dedicated user that we will use to make connections from our Notes application and that is able to operate exclusively on the notes database. Before proceeding, we remove the anonymous localhost access provided by default in Cloud SQL instances; this is a good security practice and avoids the anonymous user to shadow regular users when MySQL checks for user permissions. From the client, we issue the statement:

```
mysql> DROP USER ''@localhost;
Query OK, 0 rows affected (0.17 sec)
```

We then proceed creating a regular user:

```
mysql> CREATE USER 'notes'@'%' IDENTIFIED BY 'notes_password';
Query OK, 0 rows affected (1.47 sec)
```

Of course, we should pick up a stronger password; anyway, we have just created a new user named notes who will be able to perform connections from any host (notice the % character that is a wildcard matching any host). For convenience, we grant to the notes user any privilege on the notes database:

```
mysql> GRANT ALL PRIVILEGES ON notes.* TO 'notes'@'%';
Query OK, 0 rows affected (0.49 sec)
```

We finally make MySQL server reload all the updated privileges with the following statement:

```
mysql> FLUSH PRIVILEGES;
Query OK, 0 rows affected (0.17 sec)
```

We can now disconnect from the server, ending the current session with the `\q` command and try to reconnect using the `notes` user:

```
mysql> \q
Bye


mysql -host=<your instance IP> --user=notes -password
```

We should establish a connection with the MySQL monitor without errors, and then we can check whether we can actually access the `notes` database:

```
mysql> use notes;
Database changed
```

We can now proceed with creating tables for storing data in our Notes application.

Creating tables

Suppose we want to log users activities and store this information on a database so that we can use them later for, let's say, business intelligence analysis. Using Datastore for this purpose is not a good idea for at least two reasons:

- We will likely end with writing a lot of data, thus we cannot use too many indexes and we might have to refrain from using grouped entities.
- We will require another App Engine application to retrieve and analyze data because we cannot access Datastore from outside the platform.

Cloud SQL can solve both the issues above, respectively:

- Writing limits for Cloud SQL are far more loose than Datastore.
- We can connect to the Cloud SQL instance from an external application and access data.

We can now start defining the data we want to log; for a simple usage analysis, we can save the user identifier, the type of operation performed, and the date and time of such an operation. Once connected to the server with the MySQL client, we can issue the CREATE statement:

```
CREATE TABLE 'notes'.'ops'
(
    'id'        INT NOT NULL auto_increment,
    'user_id'   VARCHAR(128) NOT NULL,
    'operation' VARCHAR(16) NOT NULL,
    'date'      DATETIME NOT NULL,
    PRIMARY KEY ('id')
);
```

If the query succeeded, we should see something like this output:

```
Query OK, 0 rows affected (0.55 sec)
```

The SQL statement creates a relation or table named ops inside the notes database. The table has 4 columns:

- **The id column** This contains integer values that increment automatically every time a new row is inserted; this is the primary key.
- **The user_id column**: This holds the user identifier provided by App Engine, which is usually 56 characters long; we set 128 as the length so that we have room if the length grows.
- **The operation column**: This is to store the type of operation logged; 16 characters should be more than enough.
- **The date column**: This holds the date and time when operation was logged.

Connecting to the instance from our application

To connect with Cloud SQL instances from our Python code, we use the MySQLdb package, which is a MySQL driver that implements the Python Database API as described in the **PEP 249** document. To install the package, we can use pip; from the command line, we issue the following command:

```
pip install MySQL-python
```

We don't specify the `-t` option as we did when installing GCS Client Library in *Chapter 3, Storing and Processing Users' Data* because the `MySQLdb` package is included in App Engine Python Runtime Environment on the production servers and we don't need to upload it during deployment. Instead, we list the package in the `libraries` section of the `app.yaml` file:

```
libraries:
- name: webapp2
  version: "2.5.2"

- name: jinja2
  version: latest

- name: MySQLdb
  version: latest
```

A simple test to check if the database connection is working correctly consists of retrieving and logging the Cloud SQL version number. We add a function to the `utils.py` module to retrieve a connection to the database. We first need to import the `MySQLdb` package at the top of our `utils.py` module along with the `os` module:

```
import os
import MySQLdb
```

Then, we add the following function:

```
def get_cloudsql_db():
    db_ip = os.getenv('CLOUD_SQL_IP')
    db_user = os.getenv('CLOUD_SQL_USER')
    db_pass = os.getenv('CLOUD_SQL_PASS')
    return MySQLdb.connect(host=db_ip, db='notes',
                           user=db_user, passwd=db_pass)
```

The function returns a connection to the database. We retrieve all the information to perform the connection accessing some environment variables so that they are easily available from any point in our codebase. To define environment variables, we just have to add this at the bottom of our `app.yaml` file:

```
env_variables:
  CLOUD_SQL_IP: '<your_instance_ip>'
  CLOUD_SQL_USER: 'notes'
  CLOUD_SQL_PASS: 'notes_password'
```

We can use the database connection to get the MySQL version in the `get()` method of the `MainHandler` class in the `main.py` module. We first import the `get_cloudsql_db()` method and the `logging` module:

```
from utils import get_cloudsql_db
import logging
```

We modify the `get()` method as follows:

```
def get(self):
    user = users.get_current_user()
    if user is not None:
        db = get_cloudsql_db()
        ver = db.get_server_info()
        logging.info("Cloud SQL version: {}".format(ver))
        logout_url = users.create_logout_url(self.request.uri)
        template_context = {
            'user': user.nickname(),
            'logout_url': logout_url,
        }
        self.response.out.write(
            self._render_template('main.html', template_context))
    else:
        login_url = users.create_login_url(self.request.uri)
        self.redirect(login_url)
```

We can run the Notes application with the local development server and access the main page with our browser; if everything is okay, we should see a message in the log console (or in your shell if you launched the `dev_appserver.py` server from there) similar to this:

```
INFO     2014-09-28 12:40:41,796 main.py:109] Cloud SQL version: 5.5.38
```

So far so good, but if we try to deploy the application on App Engine, the result will be an error page with this error:

OperationalError: (2004, "Can't create TCP/IP socket (-1)")

This is because we are trying to access the Cloud SQL instance using a TCP/IP socket, which is perfectly fine if we connect from outside App Engine; due to the runtime environment networking restriction though, if we connect from an App Engine application, we have to use a Unix socket instead.

We can change the connection string in the `utils.py` module as follows:

```
def get_cloudsql_db():
    db_user = os.getenv('CLOUD_SQL_USER')
    db_pass = os.getenv('CLOUD_SQL_PASS')
    instance_id = os.getenv('CLOUD_SQL_INSTANCE_ID')
    unix_socket = '/cloudsql/{}'.format(instance_id)
    return MySQLdb.connect(unix_socket=unix_socket, db='notes',
                           user=db_user, passwd=db_pass)
```

We need to define an additional environment variable named `CLOUD_SQL_INSTANCE_ID` in our `app.yaml` file:

```
env_variables:
  CLOUD_SQL_IP: '<your_instance_ip>'
  CLOUD_SQL_USER: 'notes'
  CLOUD_SQL_PASS: 'notes_password'
  CLOUD_SQL_INSTANCE_ID: '<your_instance_id>'
```

If we try to deploy this version of the application, we'll notice this actually works on App Engine but it won't work on the local environment server anymore. To avoid changing the code in the `get_cloudsql_db()` function every time we switch from development to production, we can provide a method that detects automatically whether an application is running locally or on the App Engine servers. In the `utils.py` module, we add the following:

```
def on_appengine():
    return os.getenv('SERVER_SOFTWARE', '').startswith('Google App Engine')
```

This function simply returns the `True` parameter if the application is running on App Engine and the `False` parameter otherwise. We can use the function in the `get_cloudsql_db()` function in this manner:

```
def get_cloudsql_db():
    db_user = os.getenv('CLOUD_SQL_USER')
    db_pass = os.getenv('CLOUD_SQL_PASS')

    if on_appengine():
        instance_id = os.getenv('CLOUD_SQL_INSTANCE_ID')
        sock = '/cloudsql/{}'.format(instance_id)
        return MySQLdb.connect(unix_socket=sock, db='notes',
                               user=db_user, passwd=db_pass)
```

```
    else:
        db_ip = os.getenv('CLOUD_SQL_IP')
    return MySQLdb.connect(host=db_ip, db='notes',
                           user=db_user, passwd=db_pass)
```

The function will always return the right database connection for the environment our application is running on.

Loading and saving data

Now that we know how to connect to a Cloud SQL instance from our App Engine application, it's time to learn how to write and read data from the database. We already created a table called ops, and we will use it to store information about user operations. We will log the following events:

- A user has created a note
- A user has added a file
- A user has performed a shrink operation

We have to assign a text code to each of the operation types we want to log. To do so, we can use a simple Python class that works as an enumeration. In the utils.py module, we add the following code:

```
class OpTypes(object):
    NOTE_CREATED = 'NCREATED'
    FILE_ADDED = 'FADDED'
    SHRINK_PERFORMED = 'SHRINKED'
```

We will see how to use it in a moment. We now provide a log_operation() method in the utils.py module that we will use to log operations in the Cloud SQL database. We will call this function within the Notes code passing along the user who actually performed the operation, the appropriate operation type, and the date and time of the operation. The code is the following:

```
def log_operation(user, operation_type, opdate):
    db = get_cloudsql_db()
    cursor = db.cursor()
    cursor.execute('INSERT INTO ops (user_id, operation, date)'
                   ' VALUES (%s, %s, %s)',
                   (user.user_id(), operation_type, opdate))
    db.commit()
    db.close()
```

We first retrieve a valid database connection, and then we get a cursor object by calling the `cursor()` method on the connection object. By calling the `execute()` method on the cursor object, we can issue SQL statements contained in the string we pass as a parameter. In this case, we insert a new row in the `ops` table, persisting the user identifier, the string corresponding to the operation type, and the date and time when the operation was performed. We finally commit the transaction and close the connection.

We can call the `log_operation()` method from the `main.py` module at various points in the code:

- In the `post()` method of the `MainHandler` class:

    ```
    if file_name and file_content:
        content_t = mimetypes.guess_type(file_name)[0]
        real_path = os.path.join('/', bucket_name, user.user_id(),
    file_name)

        with cloudstorage.open(real_path, 'w', content_type=content_t,
                            options={'x-goog-acl': 'public-read'})
    as f:
            f.write(file_content.read())
        log_operation(user, OpTypes.FILE_ADDED,
                    datetime.datetime.now())
    self._create_note(user, file_name, real_path)
    log_operation(user, OpTypes.NOTE_CREATED,
                datetime.datetime.now())
    ```

- In the `get()` method of the `ShrinkHandler` class:

    ```
    taskqueue.add(url='/shrink',
                params={'user_email': user.email()})
    log_operation(user, OpTypes.SHRINK_PERFORMED,
                datetime.datetime.now())
    self.response.write('Task added to the queue.')
    ```

- In the `receive()` method of the `CreateNoteHandler` class:

    ```
    attachments = getattr(mail_message, 'attachments', None)

    self._create_note(user, title, content, attachments)
    log_operation(user, OpTypes.NOTE_CREATED,
                datetime.datetime.now())
    ```

Storing Data in Google Cloud SQL

Notice that by passing the date and time to the `log_operation()` method, we can record the actual time at which the user performs the operation instead of the time at which the function code was executed; this can be useful if we need to be punctual but the function is added to a task queue and executed at a later time.

From now on, when someone uses our Notes application, we will collect usage information about that user. We can access this information from the Notes application itself or another application on App Engine that is authorized to access the same Cloud SQL instance; otherwise, we can use a pure Python application that runs on our workstation or another remote server to access and process data whenever needed. For example, we create an application in an `analyze.py` module outside the App Engine project `root` (so that we can avoid uploading the file during deployment). The code is as follows:

```
# -*- coding: utf-8 -*-
import sys
import MySQLdb

CLOUD_SQL_IP = '<your_instance_ip>'
CLOUD_SQL_USER = 'notes'
CLOUD_SQL_PASS = 'notes_password'

def main():
    db = MySQLdb.connect(host=CLOUD_SQL_IP, db='notes',
                         user=CLOUD_SQL_USER,
                         passwd=CLOUD_SQL_PASS)
    cursor = db.cursor()

    cursor.execute('SELECT COUNT(DISTINCT user_id) FROM ops '
                   'WHERE date > (DATE_SUB(CURDATE(), '
                   'INTERVAL 1 MONTH));')
    users = cursor.fetchone()[0]
    sys.stdout.write("Active users: {}\n".format(users))

    cursor.execute('SELECT COUNT(*) FROM ops WHERE date > '
                   '(DATE_SUB(CURDATE(), INTERVAL 1 HOUR))')
    ops = cursor.fetchone()[0]
    sys.stdout.write("Ops in the last hour: {}\n".format(ops))

    cursor.execute('SELECT COUNT(*) FROM ops WHERE '
                   'operation = "SHRINKED"')
    ops = cursor.fetchone()[0]
    sys.stdout.write("Total shrinking ops: {}\n".format(ops))
```

```
    return 0

if __name__ == '__main__':
    sys.exit(main())
```

We can run the script from the command line at any time using the following line of command:

python analyze.py

Back to the code; in the `main()` method, we first get a connection to the database through a TCP/IP socket using the public IP of the instance. Then, we get a cursor object and perform the first query that counts the number of users we consider active, namely users who performed at least one kind of operation in the past month. As this is a count query, we expect only one row as result. In this case, we can call the `fetchone()` method of the cursor object; this method returns a tuple that contains one value that we get by index and store it in the `users` variable that we print on the standard output. With the same strategy, we retrieve and print to the standard output the number of operations globally performed in the last hour and the total number of shrinking operations.

This is just a simple example but it shows how easy it can be to get usage metrics for our web applications extracting data from a Cloud SQL instance with any Python program running outside App Engine.

Using the local MySQL installation for development

There are several reasons why we wouldn't want to work with a Cloud SQL instance while running our application locally in the development server. We might notice major slowdowns because every time we connect to a Cloud SQL instance, we perform a socket connection to a remote host that can be very far from us. Moreover, regardless of the Cloud SQL tier we choose, we always pay something for using the service and we might not want to use it while experimenting on the local development server.

Fortunately, we can leverage the fact that, in the end, a Cloud SQL instance is nothing more than a MySQL database when our code talks to it. We can then install a local instance of a MySQL server and work with this.

We install and start the local server and perform the same operations we did on the Cloud SQL instance:

1. Connect with the MySQL client.
2. Create the `notes` database.
3. Create the `notes` users and give them privileges on the `notes` database.
4. Reload database privileges.
5. Create the `ops` table.

At this point, all we have to do is change the `CLOUD_SQL_IP` environment variable in our `app.yaml` file so that it points to `localhost` variable:

```
env_variables:
  CLOUD_SQL_IP: 'localhost'
  CLOUD_SQL_USER: 'notes'
  CLOUD_SQL_PASS: 'notes_password'
```

We can now start using the local instance, avoiding network lags and costs.

Summary

In this chapter, we put into action Cloud SQL, the scalable database service offered by Google Cloud Platform. Cloud SQL is more than a MySQL instance; it is a flexible and scalable relational database server that we can use to store and retrieve data from our App Engine applications as well as from external services and applications.

Even if Cloud Datastore is the go-to solution when we have to deal with lot of data in our highly trafficked web applications, in this chapter, you learned how convenient it can be to have a relational database to store some data without hitting on the limits Datastore imposes to write operations. Being able to access that data from outside App Engine is a big plus and we have seen a simple yet effective use case, which we couldn't have implemented using Datastore.

In the next chapter, we will add new features to our Notes application; we will make the application real time using Channel API to push data from the server to the clients connected.

6
Using Channels to Implement a Real-time Application

Web applications use the request/response message exchange pattern to communicate with the server. The communication flow always starts from the client (usually a web browser), initiating a request and a server that provides a response and closes the connection immediately after. This means that if we need to get information from a server as soon as they are available, our client has to actively and repeatedly request for them using a polling strategy, which is a simple but often ineffective solution. In fact, if the poll interval is short, we need to perform a lot of requests, which consumes time and bandwidth and overloads the server; on the other hand, if the poll interval is long, we cannot consider the delivery of the information as real time anymore.

Real-time interaction between clients and servers is a requirement for a large set of web applications such as collaborative editors, online multiplayer games, or instant messaging software. In general, anytime a client needs to get information that is not systematic or predictable, similar to how it is when interacting with human users, we better go real time.

If our application runs on App Engine, we can use the **Channel** API to create an apparently persistent connection between the browsers that access the application and Google servers; this connection can be used at any time to send messages to the connected clients nearly in real time, without having to take care of the underlying communication mechanisms.

In this chapter, we will cover the following topics:

- The technology behind the Channel API
- How to implement the server part of a real-time application
- How to implement the client part of a real-time application with JavaScript
- How to deal with a client's disconnection

Understanding how the Channel API works

The Channel API basically consists of the following elements:

- **Channel**: This is a one-way communication path between the server and a JavaScript client. There is exactly one channel for each client and the server uses it to dispatch messages.
- **Client ID**: This is a string that identifies individual JavaScript clients on the server. We can specify any string as the Client ID, for example, the identifier of the current user.
- **JavaScript client**: The client is responsible for connecting to a specific channel, listening to updates on the channel itself, and sending messages to the server via HTTP requests.
- **Server**: The server is responsible for creating channels for each JavaScript client connected, providing access tokens to authenticate connections, receiving messages from the client via HTTP requests, and sending updates through the channels.

The first step for using the Channel API is delivering the JavaScript client to our users and building the code into the web pages served by the application. After the browser receives and executes the client code, the following occurs:

1. The JavaScript client asks the server with an HTTP request for a token to open a channel providing its own Client ID.
2. The server creates a channel and assigns a token to it; the token is sent back to the client.
3. The JavaScript client uses the token to connect to the channel.

Once the client is connected to the channel, the server can push messages through the channel with the JavaScript client handling them in real time, as shown in the following screenshot:

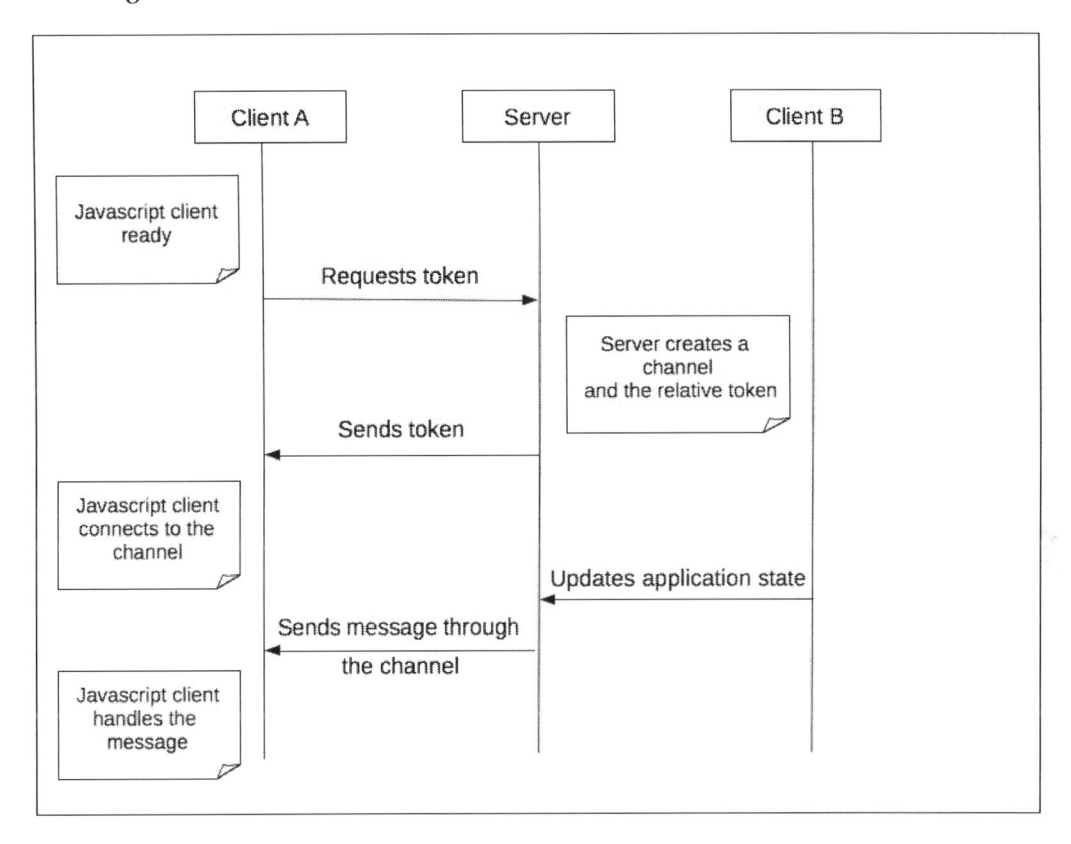

```
Client A                 Server                  Client B

Javascript client
    ready
            Requests token
            ─────────────────▶
                              Server creates a
                                  channel
                              and the relative token

             Sends token
            ◀─────────────────
Javascript client
connects to the
    channel
                              Updates application state
                              ◀─────────────────
            Sends message through
                the channel
            ◀─────────────────
Javascript client
 handles the
   message
```

We have to keep in mind two important limitations when we design an application that makes use of the Channel API:

- Only one client at a time can connect to a channel using a given Client ID; we cannot share the same channel among multiple clients.
- A JavaScript client can connect only to one channel for each page; if we want to send and receive multiple types of data from the server (for example, data regarding different parts of the page), we need to multiplex them so that all the information can flow through the same channel.

[111]

Making our application real time

To show how to use the Channel API, we will add a small feature to our Notes application. If we open the main page in a browser, there is no way for us to realize that a new note was created until we refresh the page. As a note can be created using the inbound e-mail service, it'd be nice to immediately see the change in our browser.

We are going to implement this feature using the Channel API: when we visit the main page, our application will open a channel, which will wait for new notes to be created. We will keep things as simple as possible for the scope of this book, and to avoid writing too much JavaScript code, we won't modify the **Document Object Model (DOM)** of the page; we will only show a dialog that suggests to refresh the page to see new content as soon as new notes are added.

Implementing the server

We will start by adding the Python code needed to handle channels on the server side. We expect the JavaScript client will make an HTTP GET request to request a channel, so we add a request handler that will create a channel and return a token in the JSON format to access it. We first import the modules needed at the top of our main.py module:

```
from google.appengine.api import channel
from utils import get_notification_client_id
import json
```

Then, we add the code for the request handler:

```
class GetTokenHandler(webapp2.RequestHandler):
    def get(self):
        user = users.get_current_user()
        if user is None:
            self.abort(401)

        client_id = get_notification_client_id(user)
        token = channel.create_channel(client_id, 60)

        self.response.headers['Content-Type'] = 'application/json'
        self.response.write(json.dumps({'token': token}))
```

We first check that the user is logged in and return an **HTTP 401: Unauthorized error** page if this is not the case. Then, we create a Client ID for the current JavaScript client using a `get_notification_client_id()` method that generates a string that composes the identifier of the `user` instance we pass to it together with an arbitrary prefix:

```
def get_notification_client_id(user):
    return 'notify-' + user.user_id()
```

We can add the preceding code to the `utils.py` module for convenience.

Back to the `GetTokenHandler` code; after we get a Client ID for the client, we can proceed to creating the channel by calling the `create_channel()` method and passing the identifier as the first argument. The second parameter we pass to the function is the timeout for the channel expressed in minutes; when a channel expires, an error is raised to the JavaScript client and the channel is closed. The default value when we do not specify that parameter is 2 hours, after which the client can ask for a new channel. We then set the `Content-Type` header for the response to the `application/json` parameter and finally write the token in the response body.

We finally map the `GetTokenHandler` handler to the `/notify_token` URL in our `main.py` module:

```
app = webapp2.WSGIApplication([
    (r'/', MainHandler),
    (r'/media/(?P<file_name>[\w.]{0,256})', MediaHandler),
    (r'/shrink', ShrinkHandler),
    (r'/shrink_all', ShrinkCronJob),
    (r'/toggle/(?P<note_key>[\w\-]+)/(?P<item_index>\d+)',
ToggleHandler),
    (r'/_ah/mail/create@book-123456\.appspotmail\.com',
CreateNoteHandler),
    (r'/notify_token', GetTokenHandler),
], debug=True)
```

We can check whether the endpoint is working properly by visiting the `http://localhost:8080/notify_token` URL with the local development server running. We should see something like this in the browser window:

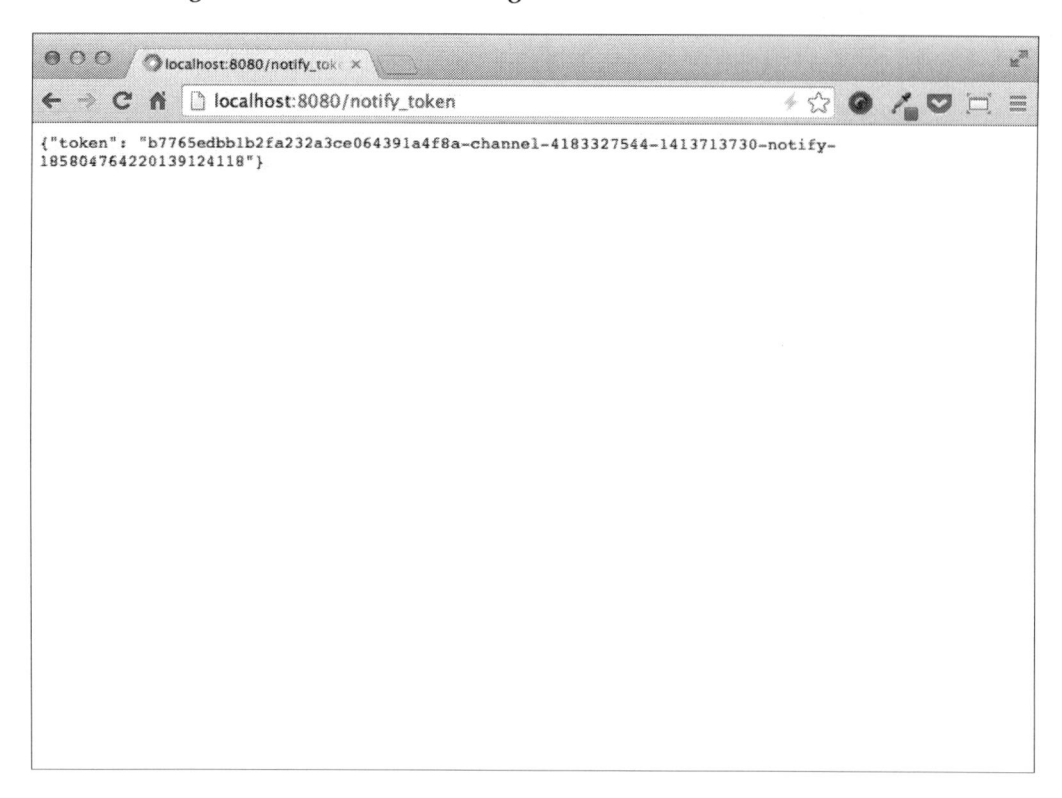

```
{"token": "b7765edbb1b2fa232a3ce064391a4f8a-channel-4183327544-1413713730-notify-185804764220139124118"}
```

The last part of the work we need to do on the server side is actually using the channels we create to send messages to our users. In particular, we want to notify a user as soon as a new note is created using the inbound e-mail service. So, we are going to add some code to the `CreateNoteHandler` handler, modifying the code of the `receive()` method as follows:

```
def receive(self, mail_message):
    email_pattern = re.compile(r'([\w\-\.]+@(\w[\w\-]+\.)+[\w\-]+)')
    match = email_pattern.findall(mail_message.sender)
    email_addr = match[0][0] if match else ''
```

```
    try:
        user = users.User(email_addr)
        user = self._reload_user(user)
    except users.UserNotFoundError:
        return self.error(403)

    title = mail_message.subject
    content = ''
    for content_t, body in mail_message.bodies('text/plain'):
        content += body.decode()

    attachments = getattr(mail_message, 'attachments', None)

    self._create_note(user, title, content, attachments)
    channel.send_message(get_notification_client_id(user),
                         json.dumps("A new note was created! "
                                    "Refresh the page to see it."))
```

After a note is actually created, we use the `send_message()` method from the channel module to send a message to a particular client. To get the Client ID of the recipient, we use the `get_notification_client_id()` method as we did before during channel creation. The second parameter we pass to the `send_message()` method is the string that represents the message we want to send to our client; in this case, we will show some simple text on a dialog in the browser as soon as the message is delivered. In a real-world scenario, we would use a more complex message than a plain string, adding some more data to let JavaScript clients identify the type and the destination of the message; this is very useful if we have to multiplex the channel to carry different information for different consumers.

We have now completed all the required work on the server, so we can move to the client side and write the JavaScript code we need to interact with the Channel API.

The JavaScript code for clients

App Engine provides a small JavaScript library that simplifies some operations needed to manage the socket connection for a channel, so the first thing we need to do before proceeding is include this code in our HTML pages. The JavaScript code must be included within the `<body></body>` tags, and we will put it just before the closing tag so that its execution will not slow down the page-rendering process.

Using Channels to Implement a Real-time Application

In our `main.html` template file, we add the following:

```
<!-- Javascript here -->
<script type="text/javascript" src="/_ah/channel/jsapi"></script>
</body>
</html>
```

The JavaScript code will be served by App Engine, both in the local development environment and in production, at the `/_ah/channel/jsapi` URL.

The code required to provide the logic for the JavaScript client will be added in a file called `client.js` that we will store in the `static/js/` path relative to the application root folder. In this manner, the file will be uploaded to App Engine servers together with the other static assets during the deployment process.

> We will write our JavaScript code inside a type of closure known as an **Immediately-Invoked Function Expression (IIFE)**, which is nothing more than a self-invoked anonymous function executed in the context of the `window` parameter as follows:
>
> ```
> (function(window){
>     "use strict";
>
>     var a = 'foo';
>
>     function private(){
>         // do something
>     }
>
> })(this);
> ```
>
> This is a common JavaScript expression most useful when attempting to preserve the global namespace; in fact, any variable declared within the function's body will be local to the closure but will still live throughout runtime.

Once we have created our `client.js` file, we need to include it within the HTML pages served by our Notes application. In the `main.html` file, we add the following:

```
<!-- Javascript here -->
<script type="text/javascript" src="/_ah/channel/jsapi"></script>
<script type="text/javascript" src="static/js/client.js"></script>
</body>
</html>
```

The order of the `<script>` tags is important because the JavaScript client must be available before executing our code.

Thanks to the functionalities provided by the JavaScript client library, we do not need to write much code. First of all, we need to retrieve the channel token from our backend, so we add the following to the `client.js` file:

```
(function (window) {
  "use strict";

  // get channel token from the backend and connect
  var init = function () {
    var tokenReq = new XMLHttpRequest();
    tokenReq.onload = function () {

      var token = JSON.parse(this.responseText).token;
      console.log(token);

    };
    tokenReq.open("get", "/notify_token", true);
    tokenReq.send();
  };

  init();

}(this));
```

Here, we declare a function named `init` that will perform an **XMLHttpRequest (XHR)** request to our backend in order to retrieve the token and will then print its value on JavaScript Console.

> Logging information on JavaScript Console is nonstandard, and it won't work for every user; this largely depends on the browser in use. For example, to enable JavaScript Console on Google Chrome, we need to perform the following steps:
> 1. Go to the **View** menu.
> 2. Select **Developer.**
> 3. Click on **JavaScript Console**.

The first instruction on the function body creates an `XMLHttpRequest` object that we will use to perform an HTTP GET request to our backend. Before firing the request, we set the `onload` callback to an anonymous function that will be executed once the response is correctly retrieved with no errors from the server. The callback function parses the text in the response body into a `json` object and logs it on JavaScript Console immediately after. After defining the callback, we initialize the request that calls the `open()` method on the `XMLHttpRequest` object and specify the HTTP method we want to use, the URL we want to reach, and a Boolean flag that represents whether we want to perform the request asynchronously or not. Later, we actually perform the request that calls the `send()` method. We then call the `init()` function itself so that it is executed the first time we visit the page and the script is loaded.

To check whether everything is working fine, we can start the local development server and point the browser to the main page after enabling JavaScript Console in our browser. If the request completed successfully, we should see the log message that contains the token on the console, as shown in the following screenshot:

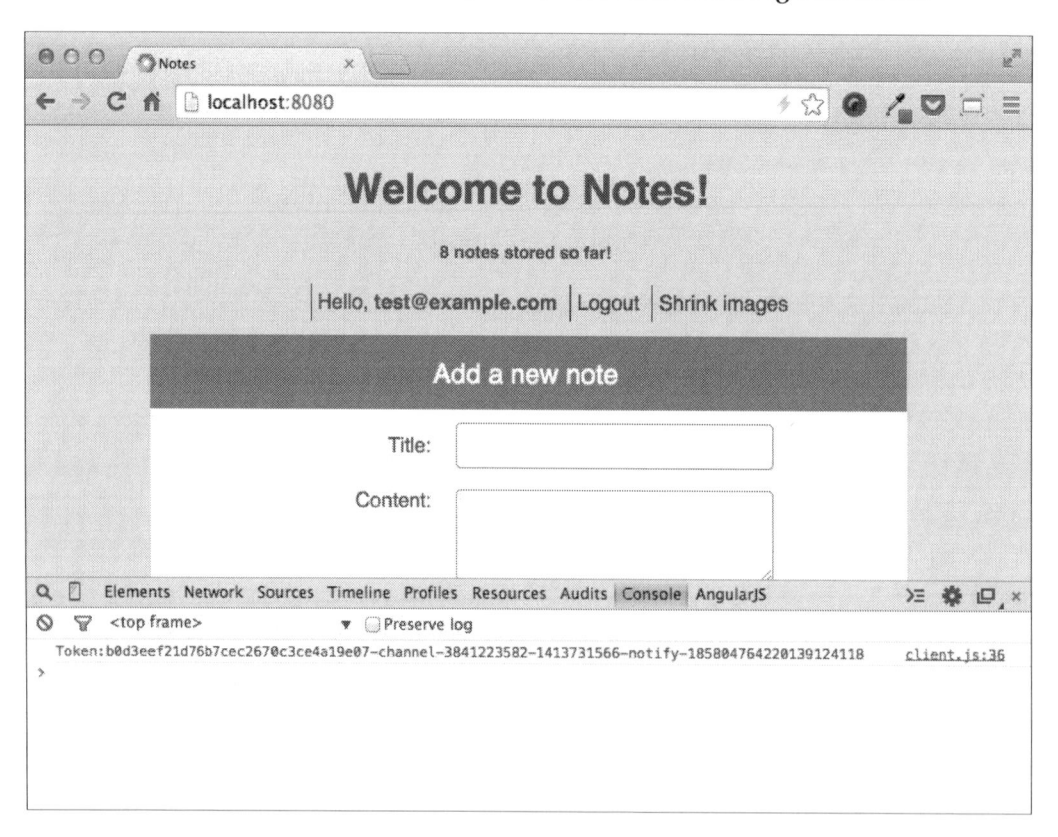

We can now use the token retrieved from the backend to open a channel. In the `client.js` file, we modify the code as follows:

```
(function (window) {
  "use strict";

  // create a channel and connect the socket
  var setupChannel = function(token) {
    var channel = new goog.appengine.Channel(token);
    var socket = channel.open();

    socket.onopen = function() {
      console.log('Channel opened!');
    };

    socket.onclose = function() {
      console.log('goodbye');
    };
  };

  // get channel token from the backend and connect
  var init = function() {
    var tokenReq = new XMLHttpRequest();
    tokenReq.onload = function () {

      var token = JSON.parse(this.responseText).token;
      setupChannel(token);

    };
    tokenReq.open("get", "/notify_token", true);
    tokenReq.send();
  };

  init();

}(this));
```

We first add a function called `setupChannel()` that takes a valid token as its only parameter. Using the JavaScript client code from App Engine, we then create a `goog.appengine.Channel` object passing the token to the constructor. We then call the open method that returns a `goog.appengine.Socket` object for the channel. The socket object keeps track of the connection status and exposes several callback functions with which we can perform operations in response to channel activities. For the moment, we only provide callbacks for the `onopen` and `onclose` socket events, logging a message on JavaScript Console. Notice that we changed the `init()` function so that it now calls the `setupChannel()` function instead of simply logging a message into JavaScript Console.

Using Channels to Implement a Real-time Application

To test whether the callbacks work properly or not, we can set a very short timeout for the channels when we create them in the backend so that we can see what happens when a channel expires in a reasonable amount of time. In the `main.py` module, we change the call to the `create_channel()` function in the `get()` method of the `GetTokenHandler` class in this way:

```
token = channel.create_channel(client_id, 1)
```

Now, if we open the main page of the Notes application in the browser with JavaScript Console open, we should see something similar to the following screenshot after 1 minute:

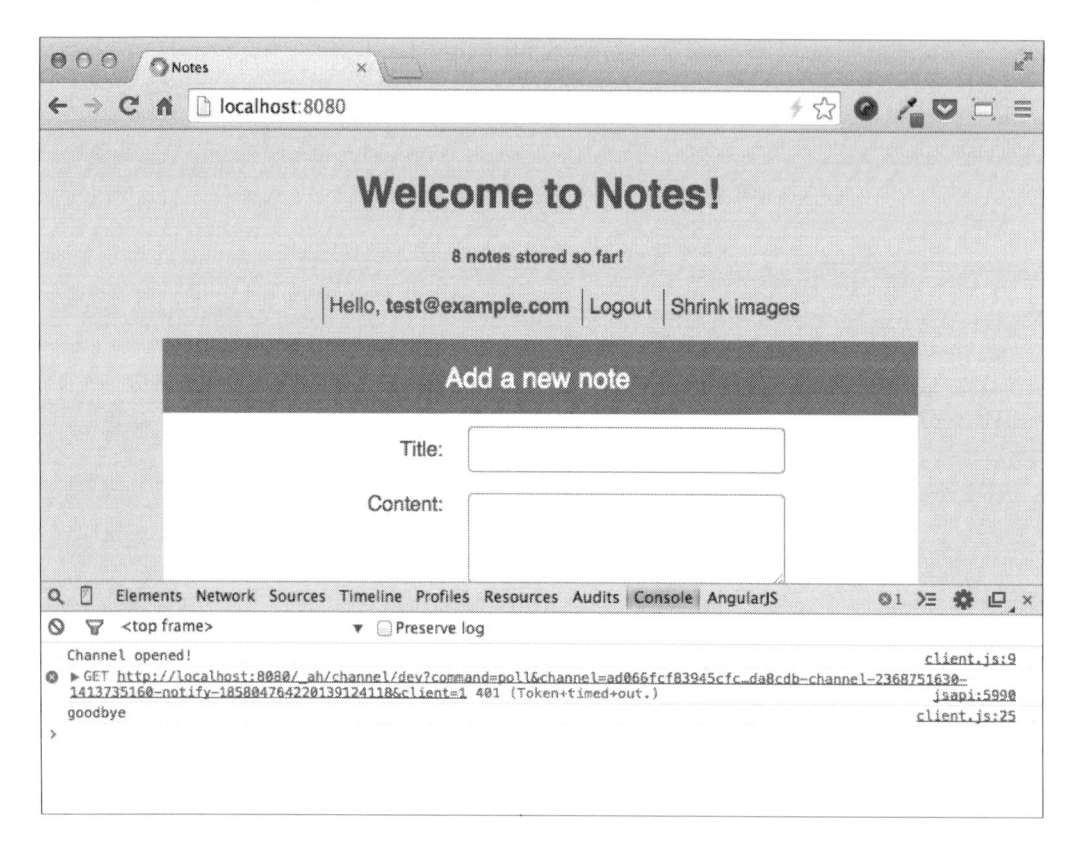

As we can see, the channel is opened and after 1 minute it expires, causing an error in the JavaScript client and finally calling the callback we set to be called for the `onclose` event of the socket object.

To deal with expiring channels, we can add a callback for the `onerror` event of the socket object. In our `client.js` file, we add the following:

```
socket.onopen = function() {
  console.log('Channel opened!');
};

socket.onerror = function(err) {
  // reconnect on timeout
  if (err.code == 401) {
    init();
  }
};

socket.onclose = function() {
  console.log('goodbye');
};
```

The callback we added is executed when an error occurs in the channel management. The callback receives an object as a parameter that contains the error message and the error code. If we receive an **HTTP 401 error** page, we assume that the channel expired and we call the `init` function to create and set up a new channel. This time, if we hit the main page and wait for 1 minute, we can see something like the following screenshot:

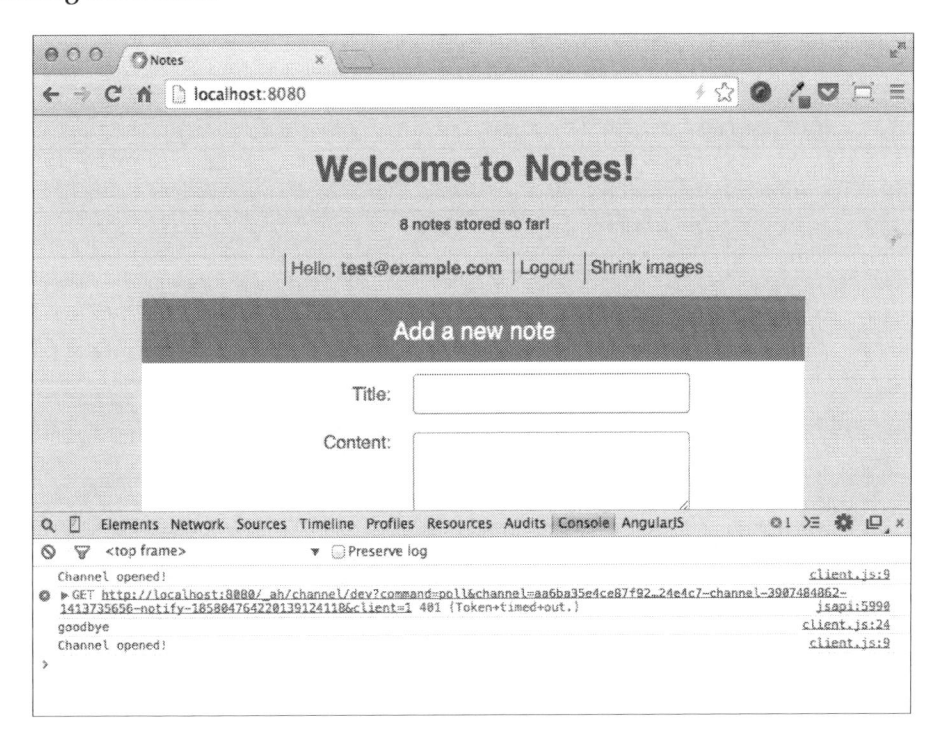

As we can see, after the channel has expired, a new one is immediately created; depending on how we use the channel, this can be completely transparent for our users.

Now, we can proceed to adding the code to handle messages pushed by the server through the channel. We have to provide a callback for the onmessage event of the goog.appengine.Socket class. When the socket receives a message, the callback is invoked and a parameter is passed: the message object. The data field of this object contains the string passed to the send_message() method on the server. We then add the following code to the client.js file:

```
socket.onopen = function() {
  console.log('Channel opened!');
};

socket.onmessage = function (msg) {
  window.alert(msg.data);
};

socket.onerror = function(err) {
  // reconnect on timeout
  if (err.code == 401) {
    init();
  }
};
```

As soon as a message arrives, we open a dialog on the browser using the alert() method of the window object. The dialog displays the string contained in the data field of the message object, stating that a new note was created and we should refresh the page to see the updated list.

To see the code in action, we can point the browser to the main page of the Notes application; then, using the local development console, we can simulate an inbound e-mail as we did in *Chapter 3, Storing and Processing Users' Data*.

As soon as the e-mail is received and the new note created, we should see something like this in our browser:

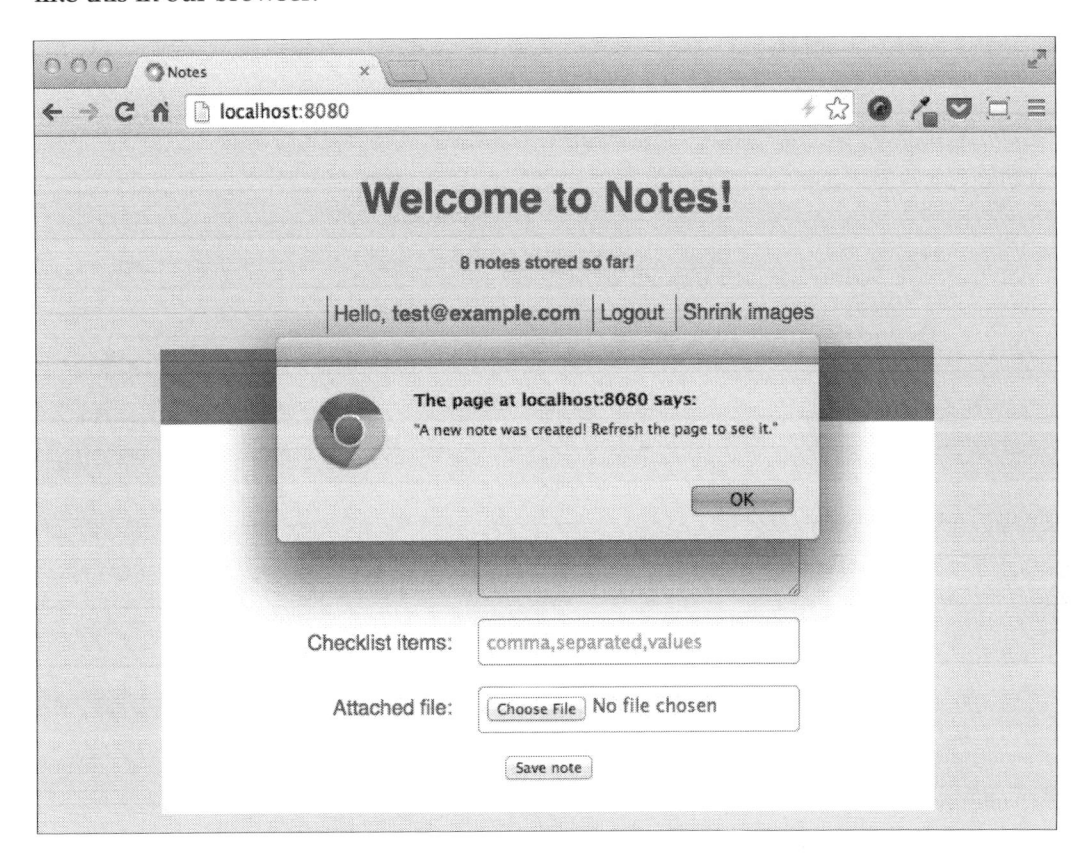

We are assuming that the only messages that arrive through the channel involve the creation of a new note, but we can send more structured data from the server; the callback function can then implement more complex logic to distinguish the content of the message and perform different operations according to this.

Tracking connections and disconnections

An App Engine application is responsible for the creation of channels and the transmission of the token, but it doesn't know whether the JavaScript client is connected or not. For example, our Notes application sends a message upon the creation of a new note through the inbound e-mail service, but on the other side, the JavaScript client might or might not receive it. In some contexts, this is not an issue, but there are several use cases where an App Engine application needs to know when a client connects or disconnects from a channel.

To enable channel notifications, we first need to enable **inbound Channel presence service**. To do this, we have to change our `app.yaml` configuration file by adding the following code:

```
inbound_services:
- mail
- channel_presence
```

Now that the `presence` service is enabled, our Notes application will receive HTTP POST requests to the following URLs:

- The `/_ah/channel/connected/` URL: When a JavaScript client has connected to the channel and can receive messages
- The `/_ah/channel/disconnected/` URL: When a client has disconnected from the channel

To see how the service works, we can add two handlers to the `main.py` module:

```
class ClientConnectedHandler(webapp2.RequestHandler):
    def post(self):
        logging.info('{} has connected'.format(self.request.get('from')))


class ClientDisconnectedHandler(webapp2.RequestHandler):
    def post(self):
        logging.info('{} has disconnected'.format(self.request.get('from')))
```

Each handler receives the `from` field into the POST request body. The field contains the Client ID of the client that has connected or disconnected from the channel. We can check out the application logs to see when the notifications take place.

Summary

In this chapter, we learned the differences between an application that uses the standard request/response exchange pattern to get data from a server and a real-time application, where the clients are persistently connected to the server and receive data as soon as it's available. Using the Channel API, we saw how easy it can be to implement a real-time web application when it runs on App Engine.

By adding a new feature to our Notes application, we should now have an idea of the features offered by the Channel API and what we can do to get the most out of its components.

We first implemented the server part, managing channel creation and message sending. Then, we moved to the client side, where we managed to implement the logic needed to interact with a channel by writing just a few lines of JavaScript code.

The Notes application is almost complete now and we have enough familiarity with Google Cloud Platform that we can stand to break it up and start over by using another Python web framework instead of webapp2. In the next chapter, we will re-implement Notes using Django.

7
Building an Application with Django

Django is an open source web application framework written in Python, originally written in 2003 by Adrian Holovaty and Simon Willison to quickly address the need for a web-based, database-driven application serving contents to an online newspaper. Django was released to the public as an open source project in 2005, and rapidly gained a strong following. With tens of thousands of users and contributors from all around the world, Django is one of the most adopted web frameworks among the Python community today, supported by an independent, non-profit foundation that promotes the project and protects its intellectual property.

One of the components that have contributed the most to the success of Django is its **Object-Relational Mapping (ORM)**, the data access layer that maps the underlying relational database with some object-oriented code written in Python. At first, what was considered a strong point of the framework turned out to be a weakness within the App Engine environment. In fact, Django provides support for relational databases only, thus excluding the Datastore option.

However, things have deeply changed after the release of the Google Cloud SQL service, and now we can use Django and its ORM with a relational database on the Google Cloud Platform. In this chapter, we will reimplement several features of the original Notes application, starting from zero and using Django instead of the webapp2 framework, showing how the App Engine platform can be a viable solution to deploy and run Django applications.

In this chapter, we will cover the following topics:

- Configuring the development environment
- Using Cloud SQL with the ORM by using the built-in authentication system
- Uploading files on the Google Cloud Storage

Setting up the local environment

At the time of writing this book, App Engine provides Django version 1.4 and 1.5 as a third-party library for the Python 2.7 runtime environment. Even though it is quite old (Django 1.4 was released on March 2012 and 1.5 was released in February 2013), the 1.4 version is currently the long-term support distribution framework, with security patches and data loss fixes guaranteed until March 2015, and the 1.5 version (thus marked as experimental on App Engine) contains a lot of new features and improvements compared to the 1.4 version. For these reasons, we can safely build our applications using one of the Django packages provided by App Engine without the risk of producing legacy code.

However, if we can afford to drop the official support that Google provides to Django 1.4 and 1.5, we can use the latest version of Django currently available, 1.7, the only difference being that we will have to take care of the deployment of the package on our own because we won't find it on the production server.

Since the deployment of applications written with Django 1.4 and 1.5 is well covered on the official documentation, and since we're building a prototype for the only purpose of learning how to get the most out of Google App Engine, we're going to develop our Django Notes application on Django 1.7; let's see how.

Configuring a virtual environment

When we need to use a specific version of Python packages that most likely differ from the ones provided by the package manger of our operating system, it's better to isolate the installation of such software in a separated environment using a tool such as **virtualenv**, and avoid clashes.

Provided we are using Python 2.7, we can install virtualenv using the `pip` package manager:

```
pip install virtualenv
```

We can now proceed to start a new App Engine application as we did in *Chapter 1, Getting Started*, by simply creating the application root folder:

`mkdir django_notes && cd django_notes`

Now we can set up a virtual environment inside the application folder:

`virtualenv .`

Every time we want to work in a virtual environment, we need to activate it before so that we can transparently use Python and pip executables to run code and install packages. For Linux and Mac OS X, we can activate a virtual environment in this way:

`source ./bin/activate`

For Windows, we can simply invoke the activation script in the `Scripts` folder:

`Scripts\activate`

To deactivate the virtual environment and stop referring to the isolated Python installation, we can issue the following command for every supported operating system:

`deactivate`

We now need to make the local App Engine Python runtime available to our virtual environment. If we followed the instructions in *Chapter 1, Getting Started*, we should now have installed the App Engine in a path on the filesystem depending on which operating system we are running. Take note of that path; for example, on Mac OS X, the App Engine SDK is sym-linked to the `/usr/local/google_appengine` URL. We then create a file named `gae.pth` and put it into the `site-package` directory of the virtual environment at the `$VIRTUAL_ENV/lib/python2.7/site-packages/` path.

The `$VIRTUAL_ENV` variable is an environment variable, available while the virtual environment is active, that points to the virtual environment installation on our local filesystem. The `.pth` file must contain the following lines:

```
/path/to/appengine/sdk # /usr/local/google_appengine on Mac OS X
import dev_appserver; dev_appserver.fix_sys_path()
```

To check that everything is working properly, we can activate the environment and try to import the App Engine package. For example, on Linux and Mac OS X, we can do this:

`source bin/activate`

`python -c"import google"`

Installing dependencies

Now that we have a virtual environment set up for our application, we can begin to install the dependencies needed to run the Django Notes application. Of course, the first package we need to install is Django:

```
pip install django -t <app_root>
```

As we have learned in *Chapter 3, Storing and Processing Users' Data*, we need to install the package with the `-t` option so that it will be uploaded to the production server during the deployment process.

Since Django is also provided by the App Engine Python SDK, we need to be sure that when we import the `import django` package, Python is actually referring to the 1.7 package in our application root folder. There are many ways to accomplish this, but we will add the following contents to the `gae.pth` file:

```
/path/to/appengine/sdk # /usr/local/google_appengine on Mac OS X
import dev_appserver; dev_appserver.fix_sys_path()
import sys; sys.path.insert(1, '/path/to/application/root')
```

Since the `fix_sys_path()` function prepends all the App Engine packages and modules to the Python path, we need to insert the path where Django 1.7 lives before anything else. That's why we're using the `sys.path.insert()` function here. To be sure that we are using the right version of Django, once the virtualenv tool is active, we can write this at the command line:

```
python -c"import django; print django.get_version()"
```

The output should be something like `1.7.1`.

We will keep adding packages as long as we need them, but we have to remember to activate the virtual environment every time we want to run the project locally or deploy the application, and most importantly, every time we install a new package.

Rewriting our application using Django 1.7

We already created the application root folder, the same folder we installed the virtual environment in. Django provides a script that builds a standard application layout called `project`, also providing some default content for the configuration file. To start a new project within the application root, we issue the following at the command line:

```
django/bin/django-admin.py startproject notes
```

We should now have a folder called notes inside our application root containing a Python module called wsgi.py we need to be aware of, as we will use it inside the app.yaml file.

As we already know, to create a new App Engine application, we need to provide an app.yaml file. We can pick any of the app.yaml files from the previous chapters as a base, and then rewrite it as follows:

```
application: the_registered_application_ID
version: 2
runtime: python27
api_version: 1
threadsafe: yes

handlers:
- url: /static
  static_dir: static

- url: /.*
  script: notes.wsgi.application
```

We changed the version number so that we can easily manage which application should run on the production server at any time: the old one built with the webapp2 framework, or the new one built with Django. We define only one handler, which will match requests for any URL and serve them using the application instance inside the wsgi.py module generated by the django_admin.py script inside our project folder.

We can now run the development server and point the browser to the http://localhost:8080 URL. If Django is working, we should see a message like this:

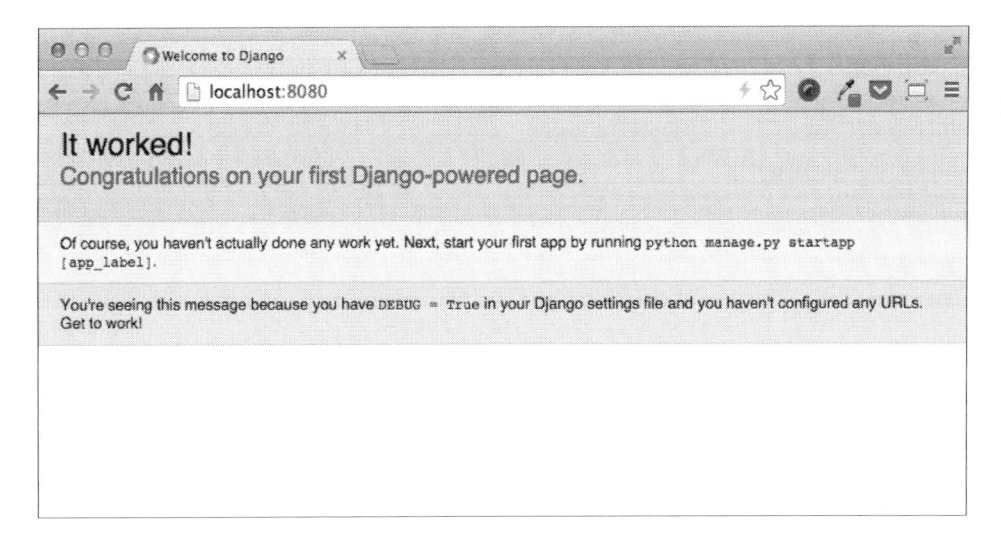

It worked!
Congratulations on your first Django-powered page.

Of course, you haven't actually done any work yet. Next, start your first app by running python manage.py startapp [app_label].

You're seeing this message because you have DEBUG = True in your Django settings file and you haven't configured any URLs. Get to work!

Building an Application with Django

As stated by the web page itself, we have created our first application on App Engine using the Django web framework. Now we can proceed and let our application do something more useful.

Using Google Cloud SQL as a database backend

We already mentioned that we will make use of Google Cloud SQL as a relational database backend so that we can run every component of the Django framework without resorting to additional packages or derived projects.

Configuring the relational database layer to make the ORM work is one of the first steps we have to take when developing a Django application. In fact, several key components, such as the user authentication mechanism, rely on a working database.

The Django ORM provides full support for MySQL databases out of the box, so all of the additional software we need in order to use Google Cloud SQL is the MySQLdb Python package, which we will install with the `pip` package manager, exactly as we did in *Chapter 5, Storing Data in Cloud SQL*. The following command is used to install the package:

```
pip install MySQL-python
```

To use the package in the production server, we have to add the following to our `app.yaml` file:

```
libraries:
- name: MySQLdb
  version: "latest"
```

We already know how to configure Google Cloud SQL, so we assume that at this point, we have an instance up and running. We can access both from the local development and the App Engine application, and we have already created a database for the project.

If we open the `settings.py` module inside our Django project folder, we will see that it contains the following:

```
DATABASES = {
    'default': {
        'ENGINE': 'django.db.backends.sqlite3',
        'NAME': os.path.join(BASE_DIR, 'db.sqlite3'),
    }
}
```

Django can use and connect to multiple relational databases at the same time from a single application, and the DATABASES dictionary contains another Python dictionary holding the configuration for each of them. For small applications, such as our Notes, we can use only one database—the one labeled default. The parameters to configure Cloud SQL when connecting from our local development environment and the parameters we need when the application is running on App Engine production servers slightly differ, so if we want to keep just one version of the settings module, we need to add some logic.

First, we need to create a utils.py module at the <app_root>/notes/notes path, containing the on_appengine() function from *Chapter 5, Storing Data in Cloud SQL*, to determine whether our application is running on App Engine or not:

```
import os

def on_appengine():
    return os.getenv('SERVER_SOFTWARE', '').startswith('Google App Engine')
```

Then we edit the settings.py module and change the DATABASES dictionary with the following code:

```
# Database
# https://docs.djangoproject.com/en/1.7/ref/settings/#databases

from .utils import on_appengine

DATABASES = {
    'default': {
        'ENGINE': 'django.db.backends.mysql',
        'NAME': 'notes',
        'USER': 'notes',
        'PASSWORD': 'notes_password',
    }
}
if on_appengine():
    DATABASES['default']['HOST'] = '/cloudsql/my-project-id:myfirst'
else:
    DATABASES['default']['HOST'] = '<instance_ip>'
```

We use the same Python database driver when we connect both from the local development environment and the App Engine production server. The database name and user credentials are also the same, but we need to specify a different HOST parameter depending on where the application is running because on App Engine, the connection is performed with a Unix socket, while in local connection, we use a TCP socket. If we want to use a local MySQL installation instead, we can change the NAME, USER, PASSWORD, and HOST parameters accordingly.

Before moving to the final step to configure the relational database, we need to introduce the concept of **migrations**, a new feature of Django 1.7. Since the ORM maps Python objects to the database schema, it will likely require altering the schema accordingly with the changes we make to the Python code. Django writes such changes to one or more migration files that reside in several `migration` folders inside our project source tree. We will see later in this chapter how to deal with migrations. For the moment, all we need to do is to invoke a command called `migrate` to create the first version of the database schema.

> To invoke Django commands, we use the `manage.py` script, which was generated by the `django_admin.py` script when we first created the project. Inside the project folder, we can launch commands in this way:
>
> `python manage.py <command>`
>
> To see the list of available commands, we can invoke the `manage.py` script without arguments:
>
> `python manage.py`

To launch the `migrate` command, we issue the following at the command line:

`python manage.py migrate`

If the Cloud SQL instance is well configured, we should see the following output:

```
Operations to perform:
  Apply all migrations: admin, contenttypes, auth, sessions
Running migrations:
  Applying contenttypes.0001_initial... OK
  Applying auth.0001_initial... OK
  Applying admin.0001_initial... OK
  Applying sessions.0001_initial... OK
```

Since the user authentication system is available by default, we can add a `superuser` user to the system with this command:

```
python manage.py createsuperuser
```

The command will prompt for username, e-mail address, and password. We can provide the credentials of our choice.

Creating a reusable application in Django

We already used the term `project` when referring to the filesystem layout generated by the `django_admin.py` script. It contains all of the code and the assets needed to run our web applications called Notes. The core of a Django project is its settings file, which defines the global environment and configurations, and we have already seen how to use it to set up the relational database layer.

It's now time to introduce the term "application." In the Django lingo, an `application` is a Python package that provides a well-defined set of functionalities and can be reused across different Django projects. We must not confuse the term "application" as defined in Django and the more general term "web application." Even though Notes is actually an application in the general sense, it is developed as a Django project and contains some functional blocks called Django applications.

A Django application usually contains the ORM model classes, view functions and classes, HTML templates, and static assets. An `application` package can be installed via the `pip` package manager or provided together with the `project` package. We need to know that a Django project will use an application only if it is listed in the `INSTALLED_APPS` settings value in the `settings.py` module.

We will create one Django application to implement Notes core functionalities, an application called `core`, to be precise. To create an empty application inside our project, we can use the `startapp` command and pass the name of the application:

```
python manage.py startapp core
```

We can see how the command created a Python package inside our project folder called `core` as we asked for. The package contains a set of standard modules we will likely want to implement, as we will see in a moment.

Building an Application with Django

As mentioned before, we need to list our newly created app inside the `INSTALLED_APPS` settings to tell Django that it must use it:

```
INSTALLED_APPS = (
    'django.contrib.admin',
    'django.contrib.auth',
    'django.contrib.contenttypes',
    'django.contrib.sessions',
    'django.contrib.messages',
    'django.contrib.staticfiles',

    'core',
)
```

Django 1.7 provides a registry called `apps` provided by the `django.apps` package, which stores an `AppConfig` object for each installed application. We can use `AppConfig` objects to introspect applications' metadata or to change the configuration of a determined application. To see the `apps` registry in action, we can access the Django shell like this:

python manage.py shell

Then we can test the following Python code:

```
>>> from django.apps import apps
>>> apps.get_app_config('core').verbose_name
'Core'
>>> apps.get_app_config('core').path
u'/opt/projects/django_notes/notes/core'
```

Views and templates

Now that the data backend is functional, we can start implementing the first building block—providing the view showing the homepage for our Notes web application. A view in the Django world is nothing more than a Python function or class that takes an HTTP request and returns an HTTP response, implementing whatever logic is needed to build the final content delivered to the client. We will add the code implementing a view to build the homepage to the `views.py` module we created inside our `core` application:

```
from django.shortcuts import render
from django import get_version
```

```
def home(request):
    context = {'django_version': get_version()}
    return render(request, 'core/main.html', context)
```

The view parameter called `home` does something very similar to the `get()` method of the `MainHandler` class in the webapp2 version of Notes. We create a `context` dictionary that will be passed to the template during the rendering process. Then we call the `render()` method, which passes the same `request` object we received as a parameter—a string containing the path to the HTML template. It will be used for the page and the `context` dictionary.

In the webapp2 version of Notes, we used Jinja2 to render our pages, but Django has its own template system already integrated in the framework. The language we use inside the HTML files is very similar to Jinja2, but some major differences still exist, so we have to rewrite our templates. We create a new HTML file at the `core/templates/core/main.html` path, relative to the `project` folder and containing the following code:

```
<!DOCTYPE html>
<html>
<head lang="en">
  <meta charset="UTF-8">
  <title>Notes</title>

  <link rel="stylesheet" type="text/css" href="/static/css/notes.css">
</head>
<body>
  <div class="container">

    <h1>Welcome to Notes!</h1>
    <h5>Built with Django {{ django_version }}.</h5>

    <ul class="menu">
      <li>Hello, <b>{{ user }}</b></li>
    </ul>

    <form action="" method="post" enctype="multipart/form-data">
      <legend>Add a new note</legend>
      <div class="form-group">
        <label>Title: <input type="text" id="title" name="title"/>
        </label>
      </div>
      <div class="form-group">
```

```html
            <label for="content">Content:</label>
            <textarea id="content" name="content"></textarea>
        </div>
        <div class="form-group">
            <label for="checklist_items">Checklist items:</label>
            <input type="text" id="checklist_items" name="checklist_items"
                placeholder="comma,separated,values"/>
        </div>
        <div class="form-group">
            <label for="uploaded_file">Attached file:</label>
            <input type="file" id="uploaded_file" name="uploaded_file">
        </div>
        <div class="form-group">
            <button type="submit">Save note</button>
        </div>
      </form>
    </div>

  </body>
</html>
```

Notice in the template how we are using the `{{ django_version }}` element, which outputs the variable we put in the context dictionary, and the `{{ user }}` element, which is provided by default by the Django authentication system. Since we did not perform a login, the current user is set to a special entity called **anonymous user**.

Now that we have a view function providing an HTTP response and a template to render an HTML page, we need to map a URL of our choice to the view, just as we did with webapp2. Django has a URL configurator module (also known as the `URLconf` module) called `urls.py`, containing pure Python code and defining a mapping between URLs described with regular expressions and view functions or classes. The `django_admin.py` script generates an `urls.py` module we can use as a starting point, but the final version to map the homepage view should be the following:

```python
from django.conf.urls import patterns, include, url

urlpatterns = patterns('',
    url(r'^$', 'core.views.home', name='home'),
)
```

A `URLconf` module must define a variable named `urlpatterns` and contain a list of `django.conf.urls.url` instances that will be iterated in order by Django until one of them matches a requested URL. When a match with a regular expression occurs, Django stops the iteration and can potentially do two things:

1. Import and call the `view` passed as parameter.
2. Process an `include` statement that loads a `urlpattern` object from another module.

In our case, we match the root URL for the domain and import the `home` function view we previously defined in the `views.py` module.

Finally, we put the same CSS file we used for the webapp2 version of Notes at the `static/css/notes.css` path, relative to the App Engine application root folder, and we should get the result for the homepage, as shown in the following screenshot:

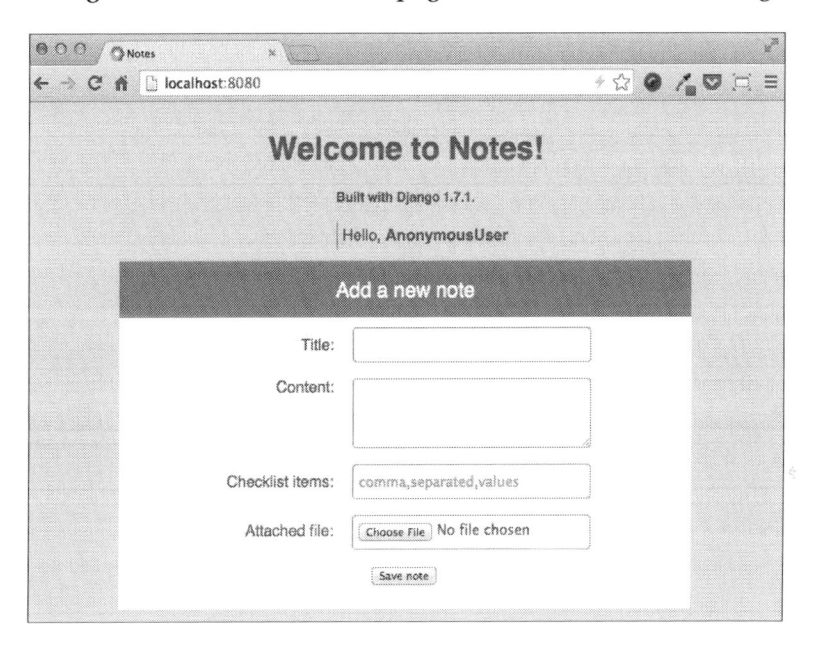

Authenticating users with Django

To authenticate our users, we won't use the App Engine User service, and we will completely rely on Django instead. Django provides a built-in user authentication system that also provides authorization checking. We can verify that users are who they claim to be, and we can determine what they are allowed to do. The authentication system is implemented as a Django application, and we have to ensure that it is listed in the `INSTALLED_APPS` settings before trying to use it as follows:

```
INSTALLED_APPS = (
    'django.contrib.admin',
    'django.contrib.auth',
    'django.contrib.contenttypes',
    'django.contrib.sessions',
    'django.contrib.messages',
    'django.contrib.staticfiles',

    'core',
)
```

The authentication system is also responsible for adding to the template context the `user` variable so that we can write `{{ user }}` in our HTML templates.

Since we won't use the App Engine User service, we must implement the login and logout pages by ourselves, and Django helps us by providing two out-of-the-box views that serve as a login and a logout page. First of all, we need to map the login and logout URLs to such views in the `URLconf` module, so we add the following to the `urls.py` module:

```
from django.contrib.auth import views as auth_views

urlpatterns = patterns('',
    url(r'^$', 'notes.views.home', name='home'),
    url(r'^accounts/login/$', auth_views.login),
    url(r'^accounts/logout/$', auth_views.logout),
)
```

Even if the logic for logging in users comes for free, we need to provide an HTML template for the login page. We add a folder called `registration` inside the `template` folder of the `core` application and create a file in it called `login.html`, containing the following code:

```
<!DOCTYPE html>
<html>
```

```html
<head lang="en">
  <meta charset="UTF-8">
  <title>Notes</title>

  <link rel="stylesheet" type="text/css" href="/static/css/notes.css">
</head>
<body>
  <div class="container">
    <form action="{% url 'django.contrib.auth.views.login' %}" method="post">
      {% csrf_token %}
      <legend>You must login to use Notes</legend>
      <div class="form-group">
        <label for="username">Username:</label>
        <input type="text" id="username" name="username"/>
      </div>
      <div class="form-group">
        <label for="password">Password:</label>
        <input type="password" id="password" name="password"/>
      </div>
      <div class="form-group">
        <button type="submit">Login</button>
      </div>
      <input type="hidden" name="next" value="{{ next }}" />
    </form>
  </div>
</body>
</html>
```

We use the same style sheet and the same page structure of the main page to show the login form. To populate the `action` attribute of the form, we use the `url` template tag, which retrieves the URL of a view whose name is given. In this case, the attribute will contain the URL mapped to the `django.contrib.auth.views.login` view. We then use the `{% csrf_token %}` template tag to create a field inside the form that Django needs in order to prevent **Cross-Site Request Forgery (CSRF)** attacks. We also add a hidden field containing the URL we want to redirect users to after a successful login. This URL is handled by Django, and the authentication system takes care of filling the `next` value in the template context.

Building an Application with Django

Our users will be automatically redirected to the login page whenever they attempt to access a URL that is login-protected. To see the authentication system in action, we tell Django to protect the `home` view by adding the following code to the `views.py` module inside the `core` application:

```
from django.contrib.auth.decorators import login_required

@login_required()
def home(request):
    context = {'django_version': get_version()}
    return render(request, 'core/main.html', context)
```

Now that we have added the `login_required()` function decorator to the `home` view, only logged-in users will be able to see page contents, and others will be redirected to the login page. If we try to access the `http://localhost:8080` URL, this is what we should see:

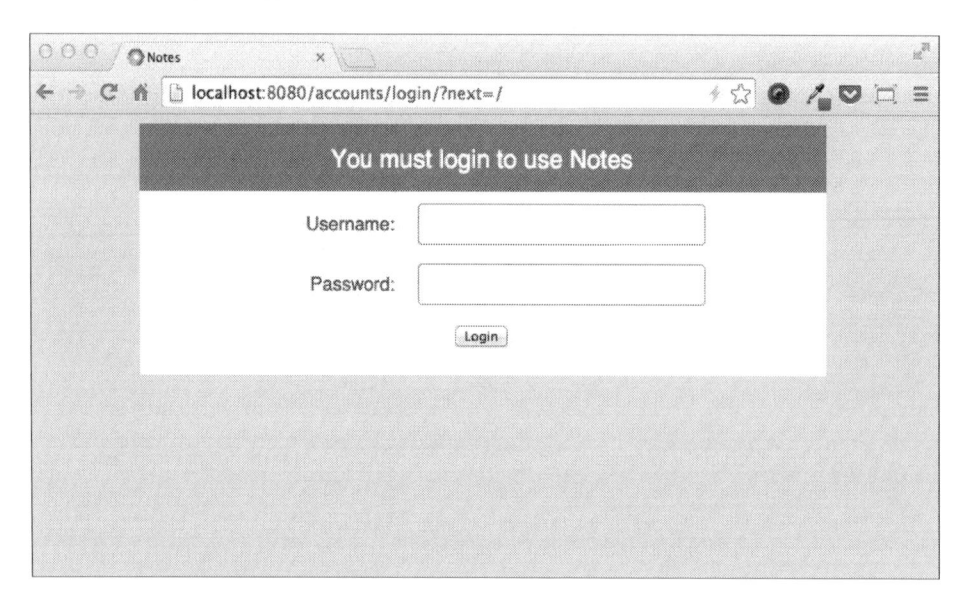

We can log in with the `superuser` user, using the same credentials we provided during the `createsuperuser` command execution earlier in this chapter.

Finally, we have to provide a link to the logout view, which users can access to terminate their authenticated session. In the `main.html` template file, we add the following code:

```html
<ul class="menu">
  <li>Hello, <b>{{ user }}</b></li>
  <li>
    <a href="{% url 'django.contrib.auth.views.logout' %}">Logout</a>
  </li>
</ul>
```

We simply retrieve the URL mapped to the logout view and Django will do the rest, performing all the operations needed to make the user log out.

Using the ORM and migrations system

We are already familiar with the model classes provided by webapp2 because in *Chapter 2, A More Complex Application*, we used them to map Python objects to Datastore entities. Django uses an almost identical approach; we define Python classes deriving from the `django.db.models.Model` package, and the ORM component takes care of mapping instances of those classes to rows and tables in the underlying relational database. To see the ORM in action, we add the following models to the `models.py` module inside the `core` application:

```python
from django.db import models
from django.contrib.auth.models import User

class Note(models.Model):
    title = models.CharField(max_length=10)
    content = models.TextField(blank=False)
    date_created = models.DateTimeField(auto_now_add=True)
    owner = models.ForeignKey(User)

class CheckListItem(models.Model):
    title = models.CharField(max_length=100)
    checked = models.BooleanField(default=False)
    note = models.ForeignKey('Note',
related_name='checklist_items')
```

We define a `Note` model class with a `title` property containing small text (up to ten characters), a `content` property containing text of arbitrary length, a `date_created` property containing date and time, and an `owner` property, which is a foreign key referring to an instance of the `User` model from the Django authentication system. Since we pass the `blank=False` parameter to the `TextField` model field constructor, the `content` property is required.

We then define a `CheckListItem` model class with a `title` property containing small text (up to hundred characters), a `checked` property containing a Boolean value that defaults to the `False` parameter when not specified, and a `note` property, which is a foreign key referring to the `Note` model. The `related_name='checklist_items'` parameter we pass to the `ForeignKey` model field constructor means that we will be able to access the set of checklist items tied to a `Note` instance accessing a property called `checklist_items` on the instance itself.

To translate our models into the SQL code needed to map them to the relational database, we need to perform a migration, more precisely the initial migration since this is the first time we are doing this for the core application:

```
python manage.py makemigrations core
```

The output of the migration should be the following:

```
Migrations for 'core':
  0001_initial.py:
    - Create model CheckListItem
    - Create model Note
    - Add field note to checklistitem
```

The `makemigrations` command creates a `migration` folder inside the `core` application path with a migration file called `0001_initial.py`. The migration file contains the list of the operations the ORM needs to perform in order to map the current Python code to the database schema, creating or altering tables accordingly.

> Migration files are part of the codebase and should be kept under version control like any other Python module.

To apply the changes to the database, we need to perform a migration with this command:

```
python manage.py migrate core
```

The output of applying the changes to the database should be the following:

```
Operations to perform:
  Apply all migrations: core
Running migrations:
  Applying core.0001_initial... OK
```

At this point, we have created the database schema for our core application. If we want to confirm exactly which SQL code was produced by the migration system, we can issue the following command:

`python manage.py sqlmigrate core 0001_initial`

This command will print on the command line the SQL code produced for our initial migration.

At this point, we might notice that our `Note` model has a `title` field that is really too small to contain descriptive titles for our notes, so we change it in `models.py`:

```
class Note(models.Model):
    title = models.CharField(max_length=100)
    content = models.TextField(blank=False)
    date_created = models.DateTimeField(auto_now_add=True)
```

Of course, this change will alter the database schema, so we need to perform a migration:

`python manage.py makemigrations core`

This time, the output will be as follows:

```
Migrations for 'core':
  0002_auto_20141101_1128.py:
    - Alter field title on note
```

A file called `0002_auto_20141101_1128.py` is added to the migration folder, containing the SQL instructions needed to alter the database schema to reflect our new Python code. The last step we need to take is to apply the migration:

`python manage.py migrate core`

Processing forms with the Forms API

Now that our database is ready to store our data, we can implement the code needed to handle the form we show in the main page to create new notes, and Django's Forms API will simplify and automate a great part of this work. In particular, we will let Django take care of the following:

- Creating the HTML form automatically from the contents of our Note model class
- Processing and validating submitted data
- Providing a CSRF security check

First of all, we implement a class deriving from the django.forms.ModelForm class that will let us define and process our form. Inside the core application, we create a new Python module called forms.py, containing the following lines:

```
from django import forms
from .models import Note

class NoteForm(forms.ModelForm):
    class Meta:
        model = Note
        exclude = ['id', 'date_created', 'owner']
```

We define a Python class implementing a so-called model form, a Django form class that defines and validates data from a Django model. We define another class called Meta inside the NoteForm class. It contains the form's metadata, mainly the name of the model it will work on and a list of fields of the model we don't want to show on the HTML form.

We will use the NoteForm class in our home view, so we add the following to the views.py module:

```
from django.http import HttpResponseRedirect
from django.core.urlresolvers import reverse
from .forms import NoteForm

@login_required()
def home(request):
    user = request.user
    if request.method == "POST":
        f = NoteForm(request.POST)
        if f.is_valid():
```

```
            note = f.save(commit=False)
            note.owner = user
            note.save()
            return HttpResponseRedirect(reverse('home'))
    else:
        f = NoteForm()

    context = {
        'django_version': get_version(),
        'form': f,
        'notes': Note.objects.filter(owner=user).order_by('-id'),
    }
    return render(request, 'core/main.html', context)
```

We initially assign a `user` variable containing the current logged-in user instance. Then we check whether the view is serving a HTTP POST request. If this is the case, we instantiate our model form class, passing the request itself to the constructor. The form will extract the data it needs from the request body. We then call the `is_valid()` method to check whether all the fields needed were filled with the right data, and we call the `save()` method passing the `commit=False` parameter that will create a new `Note` instance without saving it in the database. We assign the `owner` field to the current logged-in user and save the `Note` instance, this time making it persist in the database. Finally, we redirect the user to the homepage URL. We call the `reverse()` method and pass the view name as a parameter. If the request is of the GET type, we instantiate an empty model form. The `NoteForm` instance is added to the context so that the template can use it to render the HTML form. Here, we perform our first database query using the Django ORM. The `Note.objects.filter(owner=user).order_by('-id')` query returns a list of the notes' objects filtered by the current logged-in user as `owner` and ordered by the `id` parameter in reverse order (notice the `-` character before the field name). The list is added to the context so that the template can render it.

The final step we need to take is modifying the `main.html` template so that it can properly render the new contents we have just added to the context. Let's start with the form, which we can easily define using the model form instance, `form`, without writing too much HTML code:

```
<form method="post" action="" enctype="multipart/form-data">
    <legend>Add a new note</legend>

    {# Show visible fields #}
    {% for field in form.visible_fields %}
```

```
        <div class="form-group">
          {{ field.errors }}
          {{ field.label_tag }}
          {{ field }}
        </div>
        {% endfor %}

        {# Include hidden fields #}
        {% for hidden in form.hidden_fields %}
        {{ hidden }}
        {% endfor %}

        {% csrf_token %}
        <div class="form-group">
          <button type="submit">Save note</button>
        </div>
      </form>
```

We first iterate the visible fields of the form. Note that Django will take care of printing the correct tags and labels. After iterating through the visible fields, we print the hidden fields, then print the CSRF token (as we did for the login form), and finally provide the `submit` button. Right after the form definition, we can add the loop that produces the HTML code to show the notes to the current user:

```
      {% for note in notes %}
      <div class="note">
        <h4>{{ note.title }}</h4>
        <p class="note-content">{{ note.content }}</p>
        {% if note.checklist_items %}
        <ul>
          {% for item in note.checklist_items.all %}
          <li class="{%if item.checked%}checked{%endif%}">
            <a href="#">{{item.title}}</a>
          </li>
          {% endfor %}
        </ul>
        {% endif %}
      </div>
      {% endfor %}
```

As we can see, the `input` control to add the `checklist_items` parameter is missing. This is because we want to provide such items with the same list as we did in the webapp2 version of Notes—a comma-separated list. Since the Note model does not provide a field to hold this list, the model form won't show anything to provide such data. Anyway, we can manually add arbitrary fields to a model form independently from the fields of the associated model. In our `forms.py` module, we add the following to the `NoteForm` class:

```
class NoteForm(forms.ModelForm):
    cl_items = forms.CharField(required=False,
        label="Checklist Items",
        widget=forms.TextInput(attrs={
            'placeholder': 'comma,separated,values'
        }))

    class Meta:
        model = Note
        exclude = ['id', 'date_created', 'owner']
```

We add a new field called `ci_items`. It is not required and is rendered using a `forms.TextInput` widget. We don't use the default widget here because we want to provide the `placeholder` attribute to the corresponding HTML tag. We can refresh the homepage to see the new field appearing, without the need to touch the HTML template file. Now we need to process this new field, and we do this in the `home` view:

```
@login_required()
def home(request):
    user = request.user
    if request.method == "POST":
        f = NoteForm(request.POST)
        if f.is_valid():
            note = f.save(commit=False)
            note.owner = user
            note.save()
            for item in f.cleaned_data['cl_items'].split(','):
                CheckListItem.objects.create(title=item,
                                             note=note)
            return HttpResponseRedirect(reverse('home'))
```

After saving the note instance, we access the `cl_items` value in the `cleaned_data` dictionary Django filled after the form was processed. We split the string using the comma as a separator, create a new `CheckListItem` instance for every item the user passed through the form field, and cause that instance to persist.

Uploading files to Google Cloud Storage

By default, when users upload their files, Django stores content locally in the server. As we already know, App Engine applications run in a sandboxed environment without being able to access the server filesystem, so this approach simply cannot work. Anyway, Django provides an abstraction layer, the file storage system. We can use this layer to customize where and how uploaded files are stored. We are going to take advantage of this feature, implementing our own storage backend class that will store uploaded files on the Google Cloud Storage.

Before starting, we need to install the GCS Client Library as we did in *Chapter 3, Storing and Processing Users' Data*, in order to easily interact with the Cloud Storage from our storage backend. We then create a `storage.py` module in our `core` application, containing the definition of the storage backend class, as shown in the following code:

```python
class GoogleCloudStorage(Storage):
    def __init__(self):
        try:
            cloudstorage.validate_bucket_name(
                settings.BUCKET_NAME)
        except ValueError:
            raise ImproperlyConfigured(
                "Please specify a valid value for BUCKET_NAME")
        self._bucket = '/' + settings.BUCKET_NAME
```

The constructor must be invoked without arguments, so everything we need from within the storage backend must be retrieved from the Django settings. In this case, we expect that the bucket name was specified in the `BUCKET_NAME` settings value, and we ensure that it is a valid name using the `validate_bucket_name` parameter from the GCS Client Library. We then add to our class the methods we must provide to meet the custom storage backend requirements:

```python
def _open(self, name, mode='rb'):
    return cloudstorage.open(self.path(name), 'r')

def _save(self, name, content):
    realname = self.path(name)
    content_t = mimetypes.guess_type(realname)[0]
    with cloudstorage.open(realname, 'w',
                           content_type=content_t,
                           options={
                               'x-goog-acl': 'public-read'
                           }) as f:
        f.write(content.read())
    return os.path.join(self._bucket, realname)
```

```python
def delete(self, name):
    try:
        cloudstorage.delete(self.path(name))
    except cloudstorage.NotFoundError:
        pass

def exists(self, name):
    try:
        cloudstorage.stat(self.path(name))
        return True
    except cloudstorage.NotFoundError:
        return False

def listdir(self, name):
    return [], [obj.filename for obj in
            cloudstorage.listbucket(self.path(name))]

def size(self, name):
    filestat = cloudstorage.stat(self.path(name))
    return filestat.st_size

def url(self, name):
    key = blobstore.create_gs_key('/gs' + name)
    return images.get_serving_url(key)
```

The code is pretty much the same as what we saw in *Chapter 3, Storing and Processing Users' Data*, and all the class methods match a counterpart in the GCS Client Library, so it is very compact. Notice how in the `url` parameter we are telling Django to use the Google CDN to serve the files from our storage. We then add the following optional methods to complete our storage backend:

```python
def path(self, name):
    if not name:
        raise SuspiciousOperation(
            "Attempted access to '%s' denied." % name)
    return os.path.join(self._bucket, os.path.normpath(name))

def created_time(self, name):
    filestat = cloudstorage.stat(self.path(name))
    creation_date = timezone.datetime.fromtimestamp(
        filestat.st_ctime)
    return timezone.make_aware(creation_date,
        timezone.get_current_timezone())
```

The `path()` method returns the full path to the file, including the leading slash and the bucket name. Access to the `bucket` root is not allowed, and we raise an exception in that case.

Building an Application with Django

Now that the custom storage backend is complete, we tell Django to use it, so we write the following code in the `settings.py` module:

```
DEFAULT_FILE_STORAGE = 'core.storage.GoogleCloudStorage'
BUCKET_NAME = '<your_bucket_name>'
```

To see the custom file storage in action, we are going to slightly change the requirements of our Notes application. For the sake of simplicity, we will support only one file attached to every note so that we can simply add a couple of fields to the Note model class in our `models.py` module:

```
class Note(models.Model):
    title = models.CharField(max_length=100)
    content = models.TextField(blank=False)
    date_created = models.DateTimeField(auto_now_add=True)
    owner = models.ForeignKey(User)
    attach = models.FileField(blank=True, null=True)
    thumbnail_url = models.CharField(max_length=255, blank=True,
null=True)
```

The `attach` field is of the `FileField` type. This means Django will take care of the upload and store procedure for us, using our file storage. The `thumbnail_url` field will contain a string with the URL to retrieve the cropped version of the attachment if it is an image, just as we saw in *Chapter 3, Storing and Processing Users' Data*. It's important to remember that we have to perform a migration for our `core` application after this change. We don't want to show the `thumbnail_url` field in our HTML form, so we change the `Meta` class in the `NoteForm` file accordingly:

```
class Meta:
    model = Note
    exclude = ['id', 'date_created', 'owner', 'thumbnail_url']
```

At this point, the HTML form will show the file input field, but we need to handle uploads in our home view:

```
from .storage import GoogleCloudStorage
from google.appengine.api import images
from google.appengine.ext import blobstore

@login_required()
def home(request):
    user = request.user
    if request.method == "POST":
        f = NoteForm(request.POST, request.FILES)
        if f.is_valid():
            note = f.save(commit=False)
            note.owner = user
            if f.cleaned_data['attach']:
```

```
                    try:
                        s = GoogleCloudStorage()
                        path = '/gs' +
s.path(f.cleaned_data['attach'].name)
                        key = blobstore.create_gs_key(path)
                        note.thumbnail_url =
images.get_serving_url(key, size=150, crop=True)
                    except images.TransformationError,
images.NotImageError:
                        pass
                note.save()
                for item in f.cleaned_data['cl_items'].split(','):
                    CheckListItem.objects.create(title=item,
note=note)
                return HttpResponseRedirect(reverse('home'))
```

First of all, we pass the `request.FILES` dictionary containing uploaded data to the form constructor so that it can process and validate our `attach` field. Then, if the field is present, we generate the thumbnail URL when possible and update our `note` model instance accordingly. Here, we use our custom storage class to retrieve the path to the file in the Cloud Storage. A custom storage backend class is not usually supposed to be used directly by the developer, but in this case, we can turn a blind eye and avoid code duplication. The very last step of the procedure is to show the attachment in the Notes main page, so we change the `main.html` template in this way:

```
<h4>{{ note.title }}</h4>
<p class="note-content">{{ note.content }}</p>
{% if note.attach %}
<ul>
  {% if note.thumbnail_url %}
  <li class="file">
    <a href="{{ note.attach.url }}">
      <img src="{{ note.thumbnail_url }}">
    </a>
  </li>
  {% else %}
  <li class="file">
    <a href="{{ note.attach.url }}">{{ note.attach.name }}</a>
  </li>
  {% endif %}
</ul>
{% endif %}
```

Even if this version of Notes supports only one attachment for each note, we keep the same HTML structure we used for the webapp2 version to avoid rewriting CSS rules. We will see a thumbnail if the attachment is an image and the filename otherwise.

Summary

This was a long journey through the lands of Django, and even if we don't have all the features of the webapp2 version of Notes, at this point, we do have a solid starting point to add all the missing pieces. We already know how to deal with the Cloud Platform services, and we can complete the porting as an exercise to get better at Django programming and become even more confident with all the technologies behind App Engine.

In this chapter, we learned how to start a Django project, the basic concepts behind the framework, and how to integrate it smoothly inside an App Engine application. Using Django version 1.7, we also had the opportunity of dealing with the brand new migration system and getting the most out of the Cloud SQL database service. At this point, we know how to deal with forms, a simple example showing how easy life can be with the help of a framework like Django that saves us a lot of repetitive work. Another important step we took towards the perfect blend between Django and App Engine was the integration of the Google Cloud Storage service, an excellent backend used to store the files users upload to our Notes application.

In the next chapter, we will go back to working with the webapp2 version of Notes to implement a REST API through the Google Cloud Endpoints technology.

8
Exposing a REST API with Google Cloud Endpoints

In *Chapter 1*, *Getting Started*, we provided the definition of a web application, and one chapter after another, you learned to implement an application using App Engine. At this point, we know enough about the anatomy of such kinds of software to understand the differences between the backend and frontend components of a web application: the first provides logic, definition, and access to data, and the latter provides the user interface.

We did not make a clear distinction between these two components in the previous chapters, and the code we wrote so far provided both the frontend and the backend components without too much separation. In this chapter, we will tear apart the frontend component of our Notes application, implementing a standalone backend server ready to exchange data with different clients, from mobile applications to rich JavaScript clients running in a browser.

Once again, to implement our application, we are going to leverage some tools and services provided by the Google Cloud Platform, known as Google Cloud Endpoints.

In this chapter, we will cover the following topics:

- What REST is, and designing an API for the Notes application
- Using Cloud Endpoints to implement the REST API
- The API explorer tool
- Protecting the API with OAuth2

Reasons to use a REST API

Representational State Transfer (REST) is a simple stateless architecture style usually running over the HTTP protocol. The idea behind REST is exposing the state of the system as a collection of resources we can manipulate, addressing them by their name or ID. The backend service is responsible for making a resource's data persist, usually through the use of a database server. Clients retrieve the state of a resource performing HTTP requests to the server. The resource can be manipulated and sent back to the server through an HTTP request as well. Resources can be represented in several formats but we will use JSON, a lightweight, human-readable, and widespread interchange format. We can see the manipulation of a resource state a bit like a **Create, Retrieve, Update, Delete (CRUD)** system. What we are going to do is map each of these operations to a specific HTTP verb. We will perform an HTTP POST request to create a new resource, a GET request to retrieve an existing one, a PUT request to update its state, and a DELETE request to remove it from the system.

REST is widely adopted these days, mainly because it allows a strong decoupling of clients from servers, is easy to implement over HTTP, has a very good performance, can be cached, and in general, can scale very well. Exposing a REST API makes it extremely easy to provide a mobile client, a browser extension, or any piece of software that needs to access and process application data; for these reasons, we are going to provide a REST API for Notes. Using Cloud Endpoints, we'll be able to add a REST API to the existing codebase of the webapp2 version of Notes without touching the data models or the overall architecture of the application.

Designing and building the API

Before writing the code, we need to have a neat idea in mind of the resources we are going to make available through the API, the methods we will provide to manipulate such resources, and the response codes we will deliver to the clients. After designing the API, we can start write some code to implement resources representation.

Resources, URLs, HTTP verbs, and response code

Defining a resource is very similar to defining a model class in an ORM system, and it's not uncommon for them to coincide, like in our case. In fact, we will provide the following resources:

- Note
- NoteFile
- ChecklistItem

Every resource will be identified by a URL. We omit the hostname here for clarity:

- **The** `/notes` **URL**: This identifies a collection of resources of type Note
- **The** `/notes/:id` **URL**: This identifies a single resource of type Note using its ID as the discriminator
- **The** `/notefiles` **URL**: This identifies a collection of resources of type NoteFile
- **The** `/notefiles/:id` **URL**: This identifies a single resource of type NoteFile

We won't expose the `CheckListItem` resource through the API because in the underlying data model, we defined the items as a `StructuredProperty` field of the `Note` model. Since corresponding entities don't exist in the Datastore, we cannot alter the state of a `ChecklistItem` resource without altering the Note state as well. For this reason, exposing two different resources doesn't make much sense.

A client specifies a certain HTTP verb, or method, in the request header when contacting the backend server, and HTTP verbs tell the server what to do with the data identified by the URL. We need to know that, depending on whether a URL represents a single resources or a collection, a verb might have different meanings. For the URLs exposed by our REST API, we will support the following verbs:

- **The** `GET` **request**
    - **On a collection**: This retrieves a list of resource representations
    - **On a single resource**: This retrieves a resource representation
- **The** `POST` **request**
    - **On a collection**: This creates a new resource and returns its representation
    - **On a single resource**: This is not applicable and returns an error
- **The** `PUT` **request**
    - **On a collection**: This updates a list of resources in a batch and returns no payload
    - **On a single resource**: This updates the single resource and returns the updated representation
- **The** `DELETE` **request**
    - **On a collection**: This is not applicable and returns an error
    - **On a single resource**: This deletes the resources and returns no payload

Every time the server answers a request from a client, an HTTP status code is transmitted along with a possible payload. Our API will provide the following status codes:

- **200 OK**: This indicates that the request was successful.
- **204 No Content**: This indicates that the request was successful but the response contains no data, usually returned after a `DELETE` request.
- **400 Bad Request**: This means the request was malformed; for example, the data did not pass validation or is in the wrong format.
- **404 Not Found**: This indicates that the requested resource could not be found.
- **401 Unauthorized**: This indicates that we need to perform authentication before accessing the resource.
- **405 Method Not Allowed**: This means that the HTTP method used is not supported for this resource.
- **409 Conflict**: This indicates a conflict occurred when updating the state of the system, for example when we try to insert duplicates.
- **503 Service Unavailable**: This indicates that the server is temporarily unavailable. In particular, this occurs when our Cloud Endpoints application raises an uncaught exception
- **500 Internal Server Error**: This occurs when everything else has failed.

Now that the design of the API is complete, it's time for us to write some code.

Defining resource representations

We have already mentioned that both requests and responses might contain representations of one or more resources, and we have also stated that we will use the JSON format to implement such representations. Now we need to define a resource in our code, and Cloud Endpoints will take care of transforming our resources back and forth in JSON format for us. This operation is known as serialization.

Before we start coding, we need to spend some time on the Cloud Endpoints architecture so that it'll be easier to understand why we use certain Python packages or data structures.

Cloud Endpoints is built on top of the Google Protocol RPC Library, a framework implementing **Remote Procedure Call (RPC)** services over the HTTP protocol. A service is a collection of methods that can be invoked through regular HTTP requests. A method receives an object of a message type in the request and returns another message type in response. Message types are regular Python classes deriving from the protorpc.messages.Message class, while services are methods of a Python class deriving from protorpc.remote.Service class. Since Cloud Endpoints are actually an RPC service under the hood, the representations of our REST resources will be implemented as RPC messages.

We create a new module called resources.py on the application root, containing the following code:

```python
from protorpc import messages
from protorpc import message_types

class CheckListItemRepr(messages.Message):
    title = messages.StringField(1)
    checked = messages.BooleanField(2)


class NoteRepr(messages.Message):
    key = messages.StringField(1)
    title = messages.StringField(2)
    content = messages.StringField(3)
    date_created = message_types.DateTimeField(4)
    checklist_items = messages.MessageField(CheckListItemRepr,
                                            5, repeated=True)
    files = messages.StringField(6, repeated=True)

class NoteCollection(messages.Message):
    items = messages.MessageField(NoteRepr, 1, repeated=True)
```

Defining message classes is a bit like defining model classes in an ORM; we specify class attributes that correspond to each of the fields we want to use to represent a resource. Fields have a type, and their constructors take an integer parameter used as identifier that must be unique within the message class. The CheckListItemRepr class will be used to serialize the checkable items attached to a note. NoteRepr represents the note resource and is the core of our API.

We need a `key` field so that clients can have a reference if they want to get details or modify the resource. The `checklist_items` field references the `CheckListItemRepr` class, which will be nested into note representations. We represent the files associated with a note as a list of strings called `files`, containing keys for `models.NoteFile` instances. Finally, we define a representation for a collection of notes called `NoteCollection`. It has only one field, `items`, containing single-note-representations.

Once serialized, a JSON representation of a note should look like this:

```
{
    "checklist_items": [
        {
            "checked": false,
            "title": "one"
        },
        {
            "checked": true,
            "title": "two"
        },
        {
            "checked": false,
            "title": "three"
        }
    ],
    "content": "Some example contents",
    "date_created": "2014-11-08T15:49:07.696869",
    "files": [
        "ag9kZXZ-Ym9vay0xMjM0NTZyQAsSBFVzZXIiE"
    ],
    "key": "ag9kZXZ-Ym9vay0xMjM0NTZyKwsSBFVz",
    "title": "Example Note"
}
```

As we can see, the JSON representation is very easy to read.

Now that we have representations for our REST resources, we can start implementing the endpoints for our REST API.

Implementing API endpoints

As we already mentioned, our REST API will be integrated with the existing App Engine application without altering its behavior, so we need to specify a new WSGI application that will handle the URLs we map to the API endpoints. Let's start with the `app.yaml` file, where we add the following code:

```
handlers:
- url: /static
  static_dir: static

- url: /_ah/spi/.*
  script: notes_api.app

- url: .*
  script: main.app

libraries:
- name: webapp2
  version: "2.5.2"

- name: jinja2
  version: latest

- name: endpoints
  version: 1.0
```

The regular expression that matches API URLs is actually `/_ah/spi/.*`. Even if we perform requests to an URL such as https://example.com/_ah/api/v1/an-endpoint, Cloud Endpoints will take care of the proper redirects. The handler script of the API URLs points to the `app` variable in the `notes_api` module, which we are yet to create. In a new file called `notes_api.py`, we add the following code:

```
import endpoints

app = endpoints.api_server([])
```

This is the very basic scaffold for our REST API. Now we need to define the endpoints as methods of a Python class deriving from `protorpc.remote.Service` class, and append this class to the list that was passed as a parameter to the `api_server()` function.

In the `notes_api.py` module, we add the `NotesApi` class, which will contain all the endpoints needed to retrieve and manipulate note resources. Let's see how to implement the endpoints operating on collections of notes, one at a time, starting from the endpoint supporting GET requests:

```python
from protorpc import message_types
from protorpc import remote
from google.appengine.ext import ndb

import models
import resources

@endpoints.api(name='notes', version='v1')
class NotesApi(remote.Service):

    @endpoints.method(message_types.VoidMessage,
                      resources.NoteCollection,
                      path='notes',
                      http_method='GET',
                      name='notes.notesList')
    def note_list(self, unused_request_msg):
        items = []
        for note in models.Note.query().fetch():
            checkl_items = []
            for i in note.checklist_items:
                checkl_items.append(
                    resources.CheckListItemRepr(title=i.title,
                                                 checked=i.checked))
            files = [f.urlsafe() for f in note.files]
            r = resources.NoteRepr(key=note.key.urlsafe(),
                                   title=note.title,
                                   content=note.content,
                                   date_created=note.date_created,
                                   checklist_items=checkl_items,
                                   files=files)
            items.append(r)

        return resources.NoteCollection(items=items)

app = endpoints.api_server([NotesApi])
```

The decorator we apply to the `NotesApi` class, the `@endpoints.api` decorator, tells Cloud Endpoints that this class is a part of an API called notes with version v1. The `note_list()` method is decorated with the `@endpoints.method` decorator, and this method expects the following parameters, in the order given:

1. The message class used for the request. In this case, we don't expect any input, so we use, `message_types.VoidMessage`, a special message class provided by Cloud Endpoints.
2. The message class we will return in the response, in this case our `resources.NoteCollection` class.
3. The URL or path of the endpoint.
4. The HTTP method or verb supported by the endpoint.
5. A string representing the name of the endpoint.

The logic of the endpoint is simple—we load all the Note instances from the Datastore, and for each of them, we build a `NoteRepr` object. Representations are then added to a collection using the `NoteCollection` class and returned to the client.

Now we add the endpoint supporting requests of the POST type:

```
@endpoints.method(resources.NoteRepr,
                  resources.NoteRepr,
                  path='notes',
                  http_method='POST',
                  name='notes.notesCreate')
def note_create(self, new_resource):
    user = endpoints.get_current_user()
    if user is None:
        raise endpoints.UnauthorizedException()

    note = models.Note(parent=ndb.Key("User",
                      user.nickname()),
                      title=new_resource.title,
                      content=new_resource.content)
    note.put()
    new_resource.key = note.key.urlsafe()
    new_resource.date_created = note.date_created
    return new_resource
```

We name the method `note_create()` to better describe its semantics. It expects a `NoteRepr` message in the request containing the information to create a new resource, and will return a `NoteRepr` message in the response containing the resource created. The `new_resource` parameter contains the `NoteRepr` instance that arrived in the request and is used to build a new `Note` entity in the Datastore. We need to pass a user as the owner of the note, so we call the `get_current_user` method from the endpoints package. We will see later in the chapter how users can authenticate to use our API. After calling the PUT type, we can access the key of the newly created entity, so we update the `new_resource` message fields and return it to the client.

Here is the code for the endpoint supporting requests of the PUT type:

```
@endpoints.method(resources.NoteCollection,
                  message_types.VoidMessage,
                  path='notes',
                  http_method='PUT',
                  name='notes.notesBatchUpdate')
def note_batch_update(self, collection):
    for note_repr in collection.items:
        note = ndb.Key(urlsafe=note_repr.key).get()
        note.title = note_repr.title
        note.content = note_repr.content

        checklist_items = []
        for item in note_repr.checklist_items:
            checklist_items.append(
                models.CheckListItem(title=item.title,
                                     checked=item.checked))
        note.checklist_items = checklist_items

        files = []
        for file_id in note_repr.files:
            files.append(ndb.Key(urlsafe=file_id).get())
        note.files = files

        note.put()

    return message_types.VoidMessage()
```

The method is called `note_batch_update()` because it's supposed to perform updates on a collection of resources received in the request, returning no payload to the clients. It expects a `NoteCollection` message class in the input, and after performing all the updates needed, it returns a `VoidMessage` instance.

The last endpoint operating on a collection of notes is actually a handler for an error condition. In fact, performing a `DELETE` request on a collection should result in an **HTTP error 405: method not allowed** message. To respond to an API call with an error code, we can just raise a proper exception in the Python method implementing the endpoint:

```
@endpoints.method(message_types.VoidMessage,
                  message_types.VoidMessage,
                  path='notes',
                  http_method='DELETE',
                  name='notes.notesBatchDelete')
def note_list_delete(self, request):
    raise errors.MethodNotAllowed()
```

The `note_list_delete()` method just raises an exception that we still have to define. In a new `errors.py` module in our application, we add the following:

```
import endpoints
import httplib


class MethodNotAllowed(endpoints.ServiceException):
    http_status = httplib.METHOD_NOT_ALLOWED
```

We need to define our own `MethodNotAllowed` exception because Cloud Endpoints only provides exception classes for the most common HTTP error codes: `400`, `401`, `403`, `404`, and `500`.

The portion of the REST API operating on a collection of resources of type `note` is now complete, so we can move on and start implementing the endpoints operating on a single note. The path to single resources contains an argument, the resource identifier. In such cases, as well as when there's the need to pass query string arguments, we cannot use a simple `Message` class for the request, but we must use a special container, defined in the `endpoints.ResourceContainer` parameter, that wraps both the message and the arguments in the path and in the query string. In our case, since we're going to use the container more than once, we can define it as a field of our `NotesApi` class:

```
from protorpc import messages

@endpoints.api(name='notes', version='v1')
class NotesApi(remote.Service):
    NoteRequestContainer = endpoints.ResourceContainer(
        resources.NoteRepr, key=messages.StringField(1))
```

We pass the message we want to wrap to the constructor, along with the arguments we need to receive through the request path or in the query string. Each argument must be defined as a message field with a unique identifier.

We then proceed to define the endpoint that handles GET requests for a single-note resource:

```
@endpoints.method(NoteRequestContainer,
                  resources.NoteRepr,
                  path='notes/{key}',
                  http_method='GET',
                  name='notes.notesDetail')
def note_get(self, request):
    note = ndb.Key(urlsafe=request.key).get()
    checklist_items = []
    for i in note.checklist_items:
        checklist_items.append(
            resources.CheckListItemRepr(title=i.title,
                                        checked=i.checked))
    files = [f.urlsafe() for f in note.files]
    return resources.NoteRepr(key=request.key,
                              title=note.title,
                              content=note.content,
                              date_created=note.date_created,
                              checklist_items=checklist_items,
                              files=files)
```

We expect the `NoteRequestContainer` parameter in the input for our endpoint, `note_get()`, that will return a `NoteRepr` message. The path contains the `{key}` argument, and whenever the requested URL matches, Cloud Endpoint will fill the corresponding `key` field in the `NoteRequestContainer` instance with the parsed value. We then use the key of the resource to retrieve the corresponding entity from the Datastore, and finally fill and return a `NoteRepr` message object.

We raise an error when clients make requests of type POST on a single resource, so the endpoint is implemented as follows:

```
@endpoints.method(NoteRequestContainer,
                  message_types.VoidMessage,
                  path='notes/{key}',
                  http_method='POST',
                  name='notes.notesDetailPost')
def note_get_post(self, request):
```

```
            raise errors.MethodNotAllowed()
This is the code for requests of type PUT instead:
    @endpoints.method(NoteRequestContainer,
                      resources.NoteRepr,
                      path='notes/{key}',
                      http_method='PUT',
                      name='notes.notesUpdate')
    def note_update(self, request):
        note = ndb.Key(urlsafe=request.key).get()
        note.title = request.title
        note.content = request.content
        checklist_items = []
        for item in request.checklist_items:
            checklist_items.append(
                models.CheckListItem(title=item.title,
                                     checked=item.checked))
        note.checklist_items = checklist_items

        files = []
        for file_id in request.files:
            files.append(ndb.Key(urlsafe=file_id).get())
        note.files = files
        note.put()
        return resources.NoteRepr(key=request.key,
                                  title=request.title,
                                  content=request.content,
                                  date_created=request.date_created,
                                  checklist_items=request.checklist_items,
                                  files=request.files)
```

The `note_update()` method retrieves the `note` entity from the Datastore and updates its fields accordingly with the content of the request. Finally, the method returns a representation of the updated resource.

The last method we need to support for a single resource is DELETE:

```
    @endpoints.method(NoteRequestContainer,
                      message_types.VoidMessage,
                      path='notes/{key}',
                      http_method='DELETE',
                      name='notes.notesDelete')
    def note_delete(self, request):
        ndb.Key(urlsafe=request.key).delete()
        return message_types.VoidMessage()
```

The endpoint takes a request container, deletes the corresponding Datastore entity, and returns an empty payload if everything is fine.

We finally have a complete REST API to deal with note entities. Now it's time to play with it and check whether the results are as we expect.

Testing the API with API Explorer

We can test our REST API on the local development environment by running the `dev_appserver.py` script or deploying the application on App Engine. In both cases, Cloud Endpoints provides a tool that let us explore our API; let's see how.

With the local development server running, we point the browser to the `http://localhost:8080/_ah/api/explorer` URL, and we are immediately redirected to the API Explorer, where we can see our API listed, as shown in the following screenshot:

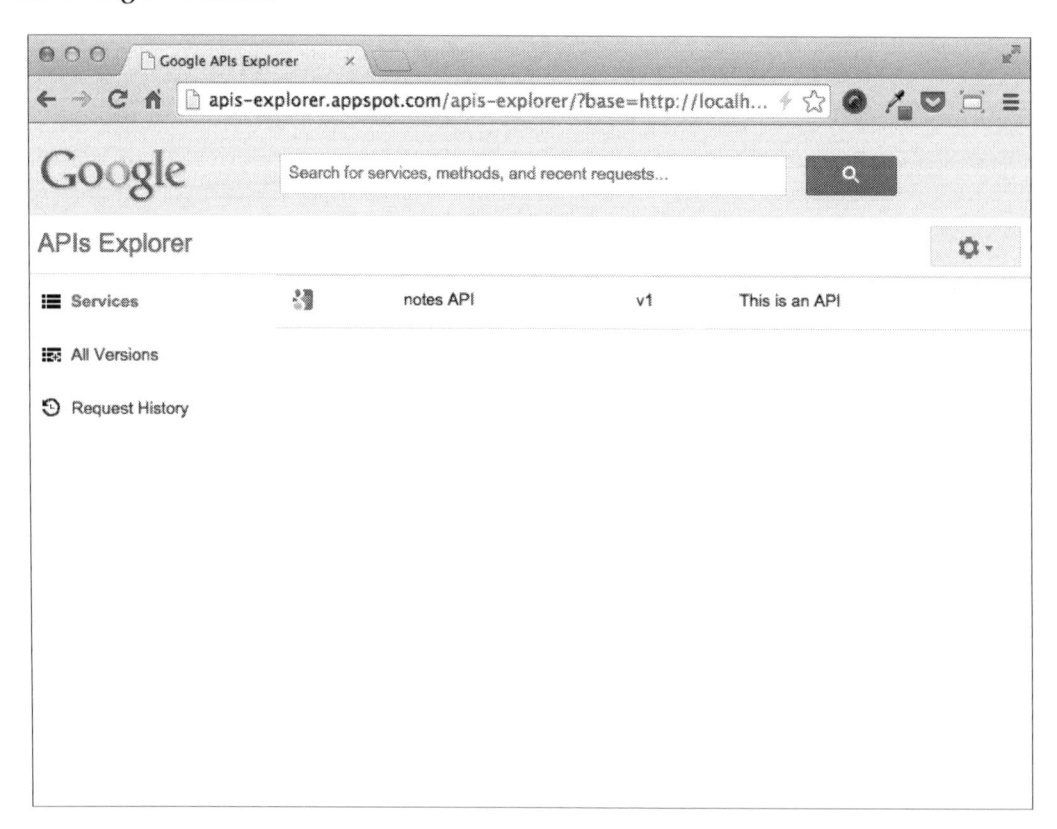

When we click on our API name, the explorer lists all the endpoints exposed through the Cloud Endpoints service. Before we begin our test, we should ensure that some notes exist in the Datastore. We can use the Notes web application to insert them.

By clicking on the notes **List** entry, we can access the details page for the endpoint, where we can click on the **Execute** button to perform a GET request and retrieve a collection of notes visible in the **Response** section, represented in JSON format. We can also copy the **key** field of one of the notes in the collection and access the details page for the `notesDetail` endpoint. Here, we paste the key on the **key** field in the form and then press **Execute** button. This time, the response should contain the resource representation.

To see how to update this resource, we access the details page for the `notesUpdate` endpoint. Here, we can again paste the key of the resource we want to update and build a request body with the **Request body** editor, a very powerful tool that let us compose complex JSON objects by just pointing and clicking on some HTML controls.

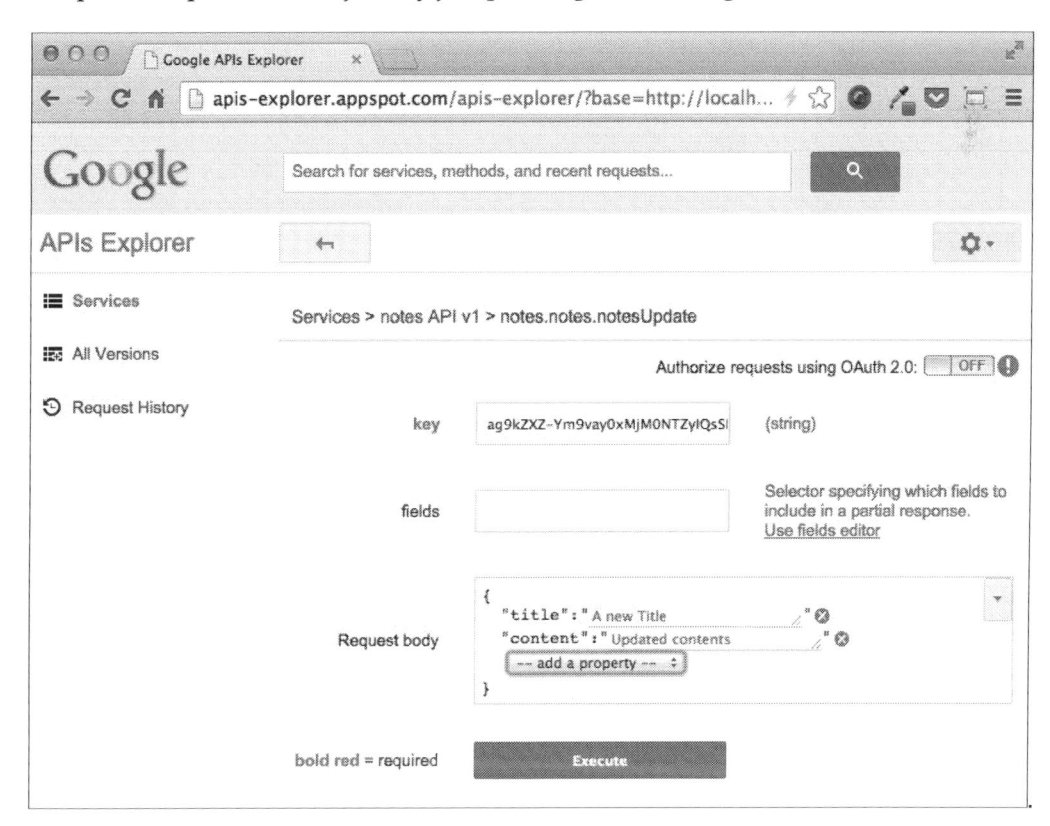

The API Explorer is of great help while developing an API to immediately see the results of a call to an endpoint, test endpoints with particular payloads in the request, and check the behavior of different versions of the same API. We could also use other clients to test our API, such as the `curl` program from the command line, but the interactivity granted by the API Explorer is a great value added.

In the next paragraph, we will see another functionality of the API Explorer that will make our lives much easier—the opportunity to test our API with a client authenticated with OAuth2.

Protecting an endpoint with OAuth2

Even if our REST API seems quite complete, a critical component is missing in our implementation: any client in fact is currently able to retrieve all the notes stored in the Datastore without providing authentication and regardless of being or not the owner of those notes. Moreover, until we don't provide authentication for our REST API, creating a note will be impossible because we need an authenticated user to create an entity in the `note_create()` method of the `NotesApi` class. We can easily fill this gap in our requirements because Cloud Endpoints provides support to protect all or part of our API with the OAuth2 authorization framework.

The first step to provide protection to our API is to specify which clients we allow to access the API. Here, we use the term "client" to actually identify a type of client, such as a JavaScript application running in a browser, a mobile application running on Android or iOS, and so on. Each client is identified with a string called client ID that we must generate using the Developer console:

1. On the left menu, choose **APIs & auth**.
2. Select **credentials**.
3. Click on the **Create new Client ID** button.

A guided procedure is then started, and all we have to do to generate a new client ID is follow the instructions on the screen.

We then specify the list of authorized client IDs with the `@endpoints.api` decorator of our `NotesApi` class, like this:

```
JS_CLIENT_ID = '8nej3vl.apps.googleusercontent.com'
IOS_CLIENT_ID = 'm6gikl14bncbqks.apps.googleusercontent.com'

@endpoints.api(name='notes', version='v1',
```

```
                    allowed_client_ids=[
                        endpoints.API_EXPLORER_CLIENT_ID,
                        JS_CLIENT_ID,
                        IOS_CLIENT_ID
                    ])
class NotesApi(remote.Service):
```

To access the API from the explorer, we also list its client ID, which is provided by the `endpoints` package. Since the client IDs are listed inside the Python source code, we have to remember that we need to redeploy the application every time we change the `allowed_client_ids` list.

If we add an Android application to the list of allowed client IDs, we must also specify the audience parameter in the `@endpoints.api` decorator. The value of this parameter is the same as that of the client ID:

```
JS_CLIENT_ID = '8nej3vl.apps.googleusercontent.com'
IOS_CLIENT_ID = 'm6gikl14bncbqks.apps.googleusercontent.com'
ANDROID_CLIENT_ID = '1djhfk8ne.apps.googleusercontent.com'

@endpoints.api(name='notes', version='v1',
                    allowed_client_ids=[
                        endpoints.API_EXPLORER_CLIENT_ID,
                        JS_CLIENT_ID,
                        IOS_CLIENT_ID,
                        ANDROID_CLIENT_ID,
                    ],
                    audiences=[ANDROID_CLIENT_ID])
class NotesApi(remote.Service):
```

The last configuration step is the declaration of the OAuth2 scopes we want a client to provide in order to access our API. For our Notes API, we will require only the `endpoints.EMAIL_SCOPE` class, the minimum required by Cloud Endpoints to provide OAuth2 authentication and authorization. We add the following to the list of parameters we pass to the `@endpoints.api` decorator:

```
@endpoints.api(name='notes', version='v1',
                    allowed_client_ids=[
                        endpoints.API_EXPLORER_CLIENT_ID,
                        JS_CLIENT_ID,
                        ANDROID_CLIENT_ID
                    ],
                    audiences=[ANDROID_CLIENT_ID],
                    scopes=[endpoints.EMAIL_SCOPE])
class NotesApi(remote.Service):
```

From now on, the Cloud Endpoints framework will automatically authenticate users and enforce the list of allowed clients, providing a valid `User` instance to our application if the authentication procedure succeeds. To retrieve the authenticated user, we call the `endpoints.get_current_user()` function the same way as we did in the `create_note()` endpoint method. If the authentication procedure fails, the `get_current_user()` function returns the `None` parameter. It's up to our code to check whether the current user is valid inside the methods we want to protect.

For example, we can add the following security check at the very beginning of the `note_list()` method in our `NotesApi` class:

```
def note_list(self, request):
    if endpoints.get_current_user() is None:
        raise endpoints.UnauthorizedException()
```

Now, if we open the API Explorer and try to perform a GET request on the `notesList` endpoint, we will get this response:

```
401 Unauthorized
{
 "error": {
  "code": 401,
  "errors": [
   {
    "domain": "global",
    "message": "Unauthorized",
    "reason": "required"
   }
  ],
  "message": "Unauthorized"
 }
}
```

Thanks to the API Explorer, we can authenticate ourselves with OAuth2 and try to access the same endpoint to check whether we are allowed this time. Staying on the page where we used to perform the failed request, we can see on the top-right corner of the API Explorer interface a switch labeled **Authorize requests using OAuth 2.0**. If we click on it, the explorer will start the authorization procedure using OAuth2 with one of our Google accounts, and once it is finished, we will be able to perform the request without authentication errors again.

Besides having authentication in place, now we can also filter Datastore queries using the user instance so that each user can only access their own data.

Summary

In this final chapter, we took an in-depth look at the Cloud Endpoints framework, and you now have the skills needed to complete the REST API and potentially support a wide variety of clients: someone could write an Android version of Notes, some other might provide a porting on iOS. We can write a JavaScript client and deliver it as a Chrome or Firefox application through their respective marketplaces.

You learned about REST in brief and why you should choose it among other solutions to talk with miscellaneous clients. We accurately designed our API, providing a comprehensive set of endpoints to retrieve and manipulate resources in our application. We finally implemented the code and played with the API using the API Explorer, an interactive exploring tool capable of executing API methods, showing request and response data, and authenticating the client.

REST is a language used in many places on the Internet, and thanks to the Cloud Endpoints, we have the opportunity to easily provide a modern and powerful API for every web application running on App Engine.

I hope you have enjoyed this book as much as I've enjoyed writing it, and whether your next Python application will be running on Google App Engine or not, I hope this book has helped you in making that decision.

Index

Symbol

_create_note() method 70

A

access
 configuring 95, 96
Access Control List (ACL) 50
action property 34
Admin Console
 URL 24, 82
ancestor query 38
anonymous user 138
API Explorer
 REST API, testing 168, 169
api_version parameter 20
App Engine
 application, uploading to 24, 25
 URL 25
App Engine Launcher 16-18
application
 Cloud SQL instance, connecting
  from 100-104
 dividing, into modules 87-90
application parameter 20
app.yaml configuration file 19, 20
attachments parameter 71

B

backup
 performing 82, 83
BigQuery 10
Blobstore API 51

B (cont.)

Bootstrap
 URL 44
buckets 50

C

Channel API
 about 109
 channel 110
 Client ID 110
 implementing 112
 JavaScript client 110
 server 110
 working 110, 111
checked property 40
checklist_items property 40
cloud computing stack
 Infrastructure as a Service (IaaS) 8
 Platform as a Service (PaaS) 8
 Software as a Service (SaaS) 8
Cloud SQL instance
 access, configuring 95, 96
 connecting, from application 100-104
 connecting, with MySQL console 97
 creating 93-95
 dedicated user, creating 98, 99
 notes database, creating 97, 98
 root password, setting 97
 tables, creating 99, 100
Cloud Storage
 files, serving from 54, 55
Cloud Storage Client Library
 installing 50
composite data
 arranging, with StructuredProperty 74-77

connections
  tracking 124
Content Delivery Network (CDN)
  files, serving through 56
  images, serving 56-58
  other files, serving 59
create_logout_url() method 33
**Create, Retrieve, Update,
      Delete (CRUD)** 156
Cron
  tasks, scheduling with 65, 66
Cross-Site Request Forgery (CSRF) 141
CSS (Cascading Style Sheets) 43
**Customer Relationship
      Management (CRM)** 67

D

data
  loading 104-107
  persisting, in Datastore 36
  saving 104-107
Datastore
  backup, performing 82, 83
  basic querying 38, 39
  caching 81, 82
  composite data, arranging with
      StructuredProperty 74-77
  data, persisting in 36
  indexing 83, 84
  models, defining 36, 37
  NDB asynchronous operations 79-81
  properties 74-77
  queries, using 77
  restore functionality 82
  transactions 40-43
  using 73
DB Datastore API 36
decode() method 71
dedicated user
  creating 98, 99
delete() method 50
Denial-of-Service (DoS) 10
dependencies, Django
  installing 130

Development Console 27
development server
  running 22, 23
disconnections
  tracking 124
Django
  about 127
  dependencies, installing 130
  local environment, setting up 128
  reusable application, creating 135, 136
  users, authenticating 140-142
  virtual environment, configuring 128, 129
Django 1.7
  used, for rewriting Notes
      application 130, 131
Document Object Model (DOM) 112
Domain Name System (DNS) 10

E

e-mail messages
  users' data, receiving as 67-71
endpoints, REST API
  implementing 161-168
  protecting, with OAuth2 170-172
entity group 38
execute_transforms() method 62

F

files
  serving, from Cloud Storage 54, 55
  uploading, to Google Cloud Storage 50
files, Notes application
  uploading, to Google Cloud
      Storage 150-153
form
  adding, to upload images 51-53
  handling 34, 35
Forms API
  Notes application forms, processing
      with 146-149
Foundation
  URL 44

G

GCS Client Library
  about 50
  installing 50
get_current_user() method 30
get_template() method 33
Google App Engine
  about 9, 11
  runtime environment 11, 12
  services 12-14
Google Cloud Datastore 9
Google Cloud Endpoints 155
Google Cloud Platform
  about 9
  Hosting + Compute 9
  services 10
  Storage 9
  URL 9
Google Cloud SQL
  about 9, 93
  using, as database backend for Notes application 132-134
Google Cloud Storage
  about 9
  Cloud Storage Client Library, installing 50
  files, serving from Cloud Storage 54, 55
  files, serving from Content Delivery Network (CDN) 56
  files, uploading 150-153
  files, uploading to 50
  form, adding to upload images 51-53
Google Compute Engine 9
Google Developer Console
  about 26
  APIs, managing 26
  applications identity, managing 26
  applications security, managing 26
  cap service 26
  Development Console 27
  filter service 26
  project members, managing 26
  URL 26

H

Hosting + Compute, Google Cloud Platform
  Google App Engine 9
  Google Compute Engine 9
HTML templates
  used, with Jinja2 31-33
HTTPS (HTTP Secure) 25
HTTP verbs, REST API
  defining 157

I

images
  serving 56-58
  transforming, with Images service 60-63
Immediately-Invoked Function Expression (IIFE) 116
in-context cache 81
indexing 83, 84
Infrastructure as a Service (IaaS) 8
installation, Django dependencies 130

J

JavaScript code
  for clients 115-123
Jinja2
  HTML templates, used with 31-33

L

Linux
  Python application, installing on 16
listbucket() method 50
long jobs
  processing, with task queue 63-65

M

Mac OS X
  Python application, installing on 16
main.py application script 21
map() method 79
mapping 78, 79

Memcache
  about 81
  using 85, 86
migrations 134
migrations system
  using 143-145
models
  defining 36, 37
modules
  application, dividing into 87-90
MySQL installation
  used, for development 107, 108

N

NDB asynchronous operations 79-81
NDB, caching levels
  in-context cache 81
  Memcache 81
Notes application
  experimenting 29
  files, uploading to Google
      Cloud Storage 150-153
  forms, processing with Forms API 146-149
  Google Cloud SQL, using as
      database backend 132-134
  migrations system, using 143-145
  ORM, using 143-145
  reusable application, creating 135, 136
  rewriting, Django 1.7 used 130, 131
  templates, creating 136-138
  users, authenticating with Django 140-142
  views, implementing 136-138
notes database
  creating 97, 98
notification e-mails
  sending 66, 67

O

OAuth2
  REST API endpoints, protecting 170-172
Object-Relational Mapping. *See* **ORM**
open() method 50

options parameter 59
ORM
  about 127
  using 143-145
owner_query() method 39

P

Packages 93
parent key 38
Platform as a Service (PaaS) 8
post() method 64
projection queries 77, 78
pull queues 63
push queues 63
Python application
  App Engine Launcher 16-18
  app.yaml configuration file 19, 20
  creating 14-19
  development server, running 22, 23
  downloading 15
  installing 15
  installing, on Linux 16
  installing, on Mac OS X 16
  installing, on Windows 15
  main.py application script 21
  uploading, to App Engine 24, 25
Python Imaging Library (PIL) 61

Q

queries
  mapping 78, 79
  optimize iterations, with mapping 77
  projection queries 77, 78
  space saving, with projections 77

R

redirect() method 30
Remote Procedure Call (RPC) 159
Representational State Transfer
      (REST) 10, 156
RequestHandler class 21

request timer 63
resources, REST API
  defining 156
  representations, defining 158-160
response codes, REST API
  200 OK 158
  204 No Content 158
  400 Bad Request 158
  401 Unauthorized 158
  404 Not Found 158
  405 Method Not Allowed 158
  409 Conflict 158
  500 Internal Server Error 158
  503 Service Unavailable 158
  defining 158
REST API
  building 156
  designing 156
  endpoints, implementing 161-168
  HTTP verbs, defining 157
  resource representations, defining 158-160
  resources, defining 156
  response codes, defining 158
  testing, with API Explorer 168, 169
  URLs, defining 157
  using 156
restore functionality 82, 83
root entity 38
root password
  setting 97
runtime environment, Google App Engine 11, 12
runtime parameter 20

S

script handlers 20
Secure Sockets Layer (SSL) 25
server
  implementing 112-115
  JavaScript code, for clients 115-123
services, Google App Engine
  about 12
  Channel API 13
  Datastore backup/restore 13

  images 13
  mail 13
  Memcache 13
  modules 13
  scheduled tasks 14
  Task Queue 14
  URL Fetch 14
  users 14
services, Google Cloud Platform
  about 10
  Google Cloud DNS 10
  Google Cloud Endpoints 10
  Google Cloud Pub/Sub 10
  Prediction API 10
  Translate API 10
set_cache_policy() method 82
Software as a Service (SaaS) 8
SQL statement
  date column 100
  id column 100
  operation column 100
  user_id column 100
static file handlers 20
static files
  using 43-46
stat() method 50
Storage, Google Cloud Platform
  Google Cloud Datastore 9
  Google Cloud SQL 9
  Google Cloud Storage 9
StructuredProperty
  composite data, arranging with 74-77
Subversion (SVN) 50

T

tables
  creating 99, 100
tasklets 80
task queue
  long jobs, processing with 63-65
  pull queues 63
  push queues 63
tasks
  scheduling, with Cron 65, 66

[179]

template context 32
templates, Notes application
   creating 136-138
threadsafe parameter 20
title property 40
transactions, Datastore 40-43

U

urlsafe() method 76
URLs, REST API
   defining 157
users
   authenticating 30
users' data
   receiving, as e-mail messages 67-71
users, Notes application
   authenticating, with Django 140-142

V

version parameter 20
views, Notes application
   implementing 136-138
virtualenv
   installing 128

W

Web Server Gateway Interface (WSGI) 11
Windows
   Python application, installing on 15

X

XMLHttpRequest (XHR) 117

Thank you for buying
Python for Google App Engine

About Packt Publishing

Packt, pronounced 'packed', published its first book, *Mastering phpMyAdmin for Effective MySQL Management*, in April 2004, and subsequently continued to specialize in publishing highly focused books on specific technologies and solutions.

Our books and publications share the experiences of your fellow IT professionals in adapting and customizing today's systems, applications, and frameworks. Our solution-based books give you the knowledge and power to customize the software and technologies you're using to get the job done. Packt books are more specific and less general than the IT books you have seen in the past. Our unique business model allows us to bring you more focused information, giving you more of what you need to know, and less of what you don't.

Packt is a modern yet unique publishing company that focuses on producing quality, cutting-edge books for communities of developers, administrators, and newbies alike. For more information, please visit our website at www.packtpub.com.

About Packt Open Source

In 2010, Packt launched two new brands, Packt Open Source and Packt Enterprise, in order to continue its focus on specialization. This book is part of the Packt Open Source brand, home to books published on software built around open source licenses, and offering information to anybody from advanced developers to budding web designers. The Open Source brand also runs Packt's Open Source Royalty Scheme, by which Packt gives a royalty to each open source project about whose software a book is sold.

Writing for Packt

We welcome all inquiries from people who are interested in authoring. Book proposals should be sent to author@packtpub.com. If your book idea is still at an early stage and you would like to discuss it first before writing a formal book proposal, then please contact us; one of our commissioning editors will get in touch with you.

We're not just looking for published authors; if you have strong technical skills but no writing experience, our experienced editors can help you develop a writing career, or simply get some additional reward for your expertise.

[PACKT] open source
PUBLISHING
community experience distilled

Google App Engine Java and GWT Application Development

ISBN: 978-1-84969-044-7　　　Paperback: 480 pages

Build powerful, scalable, and interactive web applications in the cloud

1. Comprehensive coverage of building scalable, modular, and maintainable applications with GWT and GAE using Java.
2. Leverage the Google App Engine services and enhance your app functionality and performance.
3. Integrate your application with Google Accounts, Facebook, and Twitter.

Google Apps: Mastering Integration and Customization

ISBN: 978-1-84969-216-8　　　Paperback: 268 pages

Scale your applications and projects onto the cloud with Google Apps

1. This is the English language translation of: Integrer Google Apps dans le SI, copyright Dunod, Paris, 2010.
2. The quickest way to migrate to Google Apps - enabling you to get on with tasks.
3. Overcome key challenges of Cloud Computing using Google Apps.

Please check **www.PacktPub.com** for information on our titles

[PACKT] open source
community experience distilled
PUBLISHING

Expert Python Programming

ISBN: 978-1-84719-494-7　　　Paperback: 372 pages

Best practices for designing, coding, and distributing your Python software

1. Learn Python development best practices from an expert, with detailed coverage of naming and coding conventions.

2. Apply object-oriented principles, design patterns, and advanced syntax tricks.

3. Manage your code with distributed version control.

Learning Python Data Visualization

ISBN: 978-1-78355-333-4　　　Paperback: 212 pages

Master how to build dynamic HTML5-ready SVG charts using Python and the pygal library

1. A practical guide that helps you break into the world of data visualization with Python.

2. Understand the fundamentals of building charts in Python.

3. Packed with easy-to-understand tutorials for developers who are new to Python or charting in Python.

Please check **www.PacktPub.com** for information on our titles

Made in the USA
Lexington, KY
14 May 2015